Crime

INTRODUCTIONS TO SOCIOLOGY

Crime and deviance

Johann Graaff
series editor

Frans van Aswegen
content editor

Doug Thomson
author

OXFORD
UNIVERSITY PRESS

OXFORD
UNIVERSITY PRESS

Great Clarendon Street, Oxford OX2 6DP

Oxford University Press is a department of the University of Oxford.
It furthers the University's objective of excellence in research, scholarship,
and education by publishing worldwide in

Oxford New York

Auckland Bangkok Buenos Aires Cape Town Chennai
Dar es Salaam Delhi Hong Kong Istanbul Karachi Kolkata
Kuala Lumpur Madrid Melbourne Mexico City Mumbai
Nairobi São Paulo Shanghai Taipei Tokyo Toronto

Oxford is a registered trade mark of Oxford University Press
in the UK and certain other countries

Published in South Africa
by Oxford University Press Southern Africa, Cape Town

Crime and deviance
ISBN 0 19 578078 7

© Oxford University Press Southern Africa 2004

Commissioning editor: Marian Griffin
Editor: Reinette van Rooyen
Indexer: Jeanne Cope
Designer/cover designer: Christopher Davis

Published by Oxford University Press Southern Africa
PO Box 12119, N1 City, 7463, Cape Town, South Africa

Set in 10.5 pt on 13 pt Bodoni Book by Christopher Davis
Imagesetting by Castle Graphics
Cover reproduction by The Image Bureau
Printed and bound by ABC Press, Cape Town

Contents

Introduction to the series

This small book forms part of a series of small books. The series aims to present basic sociology in a somewhat different way. First, it presents foundational sociological topics in modular form, that is each topic is presented in a separate book. That gives them considerable flexibility. Topics can be variously combined to fit a wide spectrum of introductory courses. No longer will you need to buy a hugely expensive 400-page textbook of which you only use one quarter of the available chapters. With this series you can buy exactly what you want and use all of it. The first six topics will offer introductions to: sociology in general, population studies, social institutions (education and the family), poverty and development, work and organizations, and crime and deviance.

Secondly, each book is written in such a way that it tells a coherent story with a developing and cumulative theme. Too many textbooks are accumulations of vaguely related concepts containing no discernible thread or structure. Our view in this series is that logical and sequential argument is one of the prime skills students learn at university level. As such, the texts they work with must model that style, and the exercises they do must practise it. In consequence it is important not only that the style of writing be lucid, logical and organized but also that the exercises in the book be geared towards higher cognitive skills. You will see that the exercises at the end of each book are carefully constructed to test a range of thinking skills. At the same time, there is absolutely no reason why such discussions cannot be clear and accessible, written in language that flows and entertains as it educates. Annotated bibliographies can further this aim by indicating those existing sociological works which promote a similarly easy and rich style.

Thirdly, the various books deal with issues of some substance in sociology. They go beyond the elementary concepts which make up a particular problem area. They introduce students to debates that are current and alive in modern sociology. Clearly, an introductory textbook cannot expose its readers to the full complexity of technical argument. Texts therefore need to build up gradually a repertoire of technical language and an armoury of concepts, as is the case in any discipline. After all, you cannot simply get into a car and drive it without knowing how its controls, instruments, and signals work. But once you have the hang of it, it can become a thing of great power.

Fourthly, there are many sociology teachers who want sociology text-books to be more accessible to southern African students, to use southern African examples, and promote something called 'southern African sociology'. While sociological writing in this subcontinent without doubt benefits from the use of southern African references and examples, and this series of books certainly pursues that practice, the spread of ethnic or cultural groups and ideological convictions, makes the existence of a southern African sociology, in the singular, very doubtful. Rather we would expect a range of sociologies, in the plural. But, even then, the influence of global sociological paradigms is so powerful that it is difficult to find anything which could be called distinctively 'southern African'. So, southern African reference points and examples, yes, but southern African sociology(ies) – very difficult.

Finally, sociology is a discipline that can reveal, open up, unveil the social world around us in wondrous ways. It's like cracking a secret code. It can make unthought-of, even unheard-of, connections and links. But it can also be personal and challenging. It can put question marks behind some of your most dearly held beliefs. Going on the sociological journey, then, can be exciting, surprising, angering, outrageous, and scary. It would not be true sociology if it were not.

Johann Graaff
Series Editor

1 Introduction

This chapter answers some basic questions: What is deviance? What is crime? How do we explain their presence in society? We spell out the three foundation theories that sociologists use to understand crime: functionalism, Marxism, and symbolic interactionism.

Thandi does not like going to school. Her classmates call her names and make fun of her. She is overweight, and the other children think that she is lazy and stupid. Thandi does not try very hard at school because she does not get much encouragement from other people. It is easier for her to try to keep quiet and away from the other children. She gets very depressed and sometimes thinks about killing herself.

Tom sells drugs. He is the leader of a well-organised gang, and has been able to make a lot of money from dealing in heroin and mandrax. With the money he has been able to buy his elderly mother a house and pay for her hospital treatment, something that she could never afford.

Both these people are deviant; one is a criminal. Their reasons for being deviant are different.

The first lesson to be learned about crime and deviance, and also a central theme of this entire book, is that there is no objective or absolute definition of what deviance and crime is. Deviant and criminal acts vary hugely across societies and across historical time. It depends a great deal on the cultural context of the behaviour being studied. What is deviant in one society might be quite normal in another.

The second organising theme of this book is its three-part theoretical foundation. These parts are: functionalism, Marxism, and symbolic interactionism. This book follows the organisation of all the books in this series, and draws on the original elaboration of principles as set out in the first book of the series, entitled *What is Sociology?* (Graaff, 2002).

Thirdly, the book investigates a number of key issues in the sociology of deviance and crime. These are the issues of violence, of juvenile delinquency, of white-collar crime and finally the problem of controlling crime. Each of these is examined with a view to mobilising and illustrating the theoretical tools in this area of sociology. In the process you will see the three base theories multiplying into a variety of offshoot theories. While these retain their links to their roots, they are also often mixtures of a number of different theories. All the theories and their origins are summarised at the end of the book (see page 60).

So, let us start with two basic questions in any sociological investigation: How are we to define deviance and crime? And how do we understand where they come from?

What is deviance? What is crime? What is the difference?

The most common meaning of the term 'deviance' among sociologists is that it refers to *the violation of the norms of a society or group*. In this sense deviance is not intrinsic to specific types of behaviour, but *relative* to the norms of the society or group that is under discussion (Goode, 1997). All behaviours have at some time, in some society, been seen as normal. There are no universally deviant acts. The Aztecs performed human sacrifices. Among the ancient Egyptian pharaohs, brothers married sisters. Educating women was once deviant; so was the use of anaesthetic in operations (some believed that pain helped to heal).

The relativity of deviance also implies that what is seen as deviance varies according to the *situation* in which the behaviour occurs. Drinking three beers is generally seen as normal if you drink them in the evening with friends, but not at seven in the morning (unless you are a university student). Singing loudly is fine if you are in the bath, but not if you are in a queue in the post office. In this case, people might not do much more than laugh and shake their heads.

But when behaviour is considered to be dangerous or threatening to the society, then that deviant act and the person doing the act (the actor) will be seen as harmfully deviant. It is in such instances that the state usually decides to define the behaviour as a *crime* that should be handled and punished within the state's criminal justice system (police, courts, correctional service) as is the case with rape, murder, assault, robbery, and burglary, for example. *Crimes are therefore violations of a specific subtype of norms, that is, the criminal laws of a society.* In certain instances there is also provision that certain types of behaviour are viewed as criminal in terms of international agreements. War crimes are an example. In such instances individuals accused of war crimes will be prosecuted by an international tribunal.

> All behaviours have at some time, in some society, been seen as normal. There are no universally deviant acts.

Before departing from the notion of deviance, we need to make four further qualifications.

Firstly, when the term deviance is used, it most commonly refers to types of *behaviour* that violate the norms. But remember that it can also refer to political and religious beliefs and to physical *attributes* that people display (Higgins and Butler, 1982).

Secondly, behaviour that is *statistically rare* in a society or group is not necessarily deviant. If you are the tallest person or the only male or the only one who studied for the exam in a group, you differ from the norm or average (medium height, female, did not study). In this case you are not deviant. You are just different. Being different, however, becomes deviant when society disapproves of your difference. It is society's opinion of what you do that constitutes deviance.

Being different, however, becomes deviant when society disapproves of your difference.

Thirdly, to define deviance as behaviour that violates the norms of a society or group has the implication that an extremely wide variety of behaviours qualify as deviant. *In practice* sociologists concentrate more on the study of deviance that is seen as a major social problem. This includes violating societal norms related to respect for other people's lives and their property, as well as behaviour such as suicide and drug addiction.

Lastly, the dominant norms and laws are not necessarily those of the majority of society. Instead, they are more frequently the norms and laws of those who are *powerful* in society. The rules which one is required to follow in society, which in effect determine what is normal and what is deviant, might then be those imposed by a smaller section of society.

Studying deviance and crime in South Africa is not only intriguing, but also highly complex. Here are some more examples:

'A 13 year-old African baby-sitter appeared in court on a charge of assault because he hugged a white child in his charge. He had knelt down and opened his arms, and the little girl had run to him and they had hugged.' *(Frontline, April 1985)*

'The police report to the Paarl Liquor Licensing Board issued yesterday emphasises that in all cases glasses for Whites and non-whites are to be washed separately and kept apart. Separate cloths must also be used for drying the glasses and kept apart.' *(Cape Times, 21 October 1960)*

'Mata Beula, 36, was fined R30 (or two months) in the East-London Magistrate's Court this week for stealing one banana. The value of the banana was placed at one cent. It was his first conviction.' *(Sunday Times, 12 March 1961)*

Let us turn our attention now to understanding why people deviate and commit crime.

Functionalists believe
that societies tend to
be stable and orderly.

Theories and explanations

Consider the following quite common statements about crime. Do you
agree or disagree with them?

1 If there were no punishment, people would commit more crime.
2 Some people are born criminals.
3 If your friends and family are deviant, then you will be.
4 If someone is always treated as a criminal, he or she will become a
   criminal.
5 People are criminals because of their poor education and lack of work
   opportunities.
6 The whole justice system is designed to protect the rich and powerful
   and punish the poor and weak.
7 The justice system discriminates against women.

The way you responded to these statements shows how you believe crime
and deviance are caused, and thus how they can be reduced. Each statement reflects a particular theory of deviance and, as you can see, they do
not agree on the causes. Let us consider our three types of theory.

Functionalism

Functionalists believe that societies tend to be stable and orderly. Their
research focuses on showing how social order is maintained. Shared values and norms in a society form the basis of social order, and it is through
the sharing and reinforcement of these values that communities are able
to function. Crime occurs when the social order is disrupted.

For French sociologist **Emile Durkheim** (1858–1917), normally
social behaviour has a positive function for society. The same principle
applies to crime, as we shall see in a moment.

In traditional societies and communities, said Durkheim, informal
social controls work to maintain order. In such small-scale societies the
dominance of religion and the kinship system ensures shared values and
a strong moral order. As a result, there is less need for formal policing or
written law. As societies grow, however, so there is a need for the codifi-
cation of the values and morals into law. In modern societies the law
establishes what the boundaries are for behaviour, and the public display
of the law (in the courts) shows people what behaviour is acceptable, and
what happens to those who deviate.

Crime is a positive social force, said Durkheim. Crime tests the laws,
challenges the status quo, and brings about change. The change is not
always radical, but steady and progressive. Crime also serves to bring

people together. If a crime occurs in your community, you will share with others a stronger social bond of disapproval. If the criminal is caught and punished, then the community norms are reinforced. However, too much crime will damage a society. The normal social boundaries governing 'right' and 'wrong' will be broken, there will be no shared set of values and the social structure will be seriously harmed, a situation he called *anomie*.

One of the most influential functionalist theorists after Durkheim was Robert Merton (1910–2003). His academic career started in an era when biological and psychological explanations were dominant. Merton was critical of these theories and he was one of the first theorists to break away from this tradition in his emphasis on social factors as causes of crime and deviance.

Merton and anomie

Now Durkheim's concept of anomie relates to two of his other ideas: (i) unless regulated by society, people may become less attached to the values of society, and (ii) society should regulate people's desires because 'unrealistic' desires may result in deviance. To Durkheim the lack of regulation is caused by changes in the structure of society, for example during rapid social change.

Merton adapted these ideas in his attempt to explain why deviance occurs in modern societies, more specifically in the United States of America. He suggested societies have sets of *culturally prescribed goals* that act as legitimate objectives for all members of a society. Achieving the goals means that you will attain a certain status as part of that society. On the other hand culture also prescribes the *legitimate means* (or *institutionalised means*) that should be used to reach the goals. In America, for example, a commonly accepted cultural goal is to achieve success as measured by financial wealth. However, the legitimate means to this goal is through education and a legitimate job.

A problem arises, however, if you *do not have access to the legitimate means* to obtain the cultural goals. For Merton this mainly results from a person's *position in the social structure* of society. Your means to financial success may be blocked because you lack the correct qualifications, because you are the 'wrong' race, gender, or ethnic group, or because you live in a poor area. Individuals are thus placed under *strain* by their position in the social structure to obtain the cultural goals and it is under these conditions that people's attachment to the norms may diminish (a situation of *normlessness* or *anomie*) and they may contemplate deviance. For example, an unemployed working-class father and husband might feel embarrassed because he has a family to support and, as a man, he is

> A problem arises, however, if you *do not have access to the legitimate means* to obtain the cultural goals.

Merton used the concepts of cultural goals and institution-alised means to classify various *types* of deviance.

ashamed that he cannot look after them properly. In this case he may reject the culturally prescribed means for achieving an income, and resort to deviant or criminal means. He may also begin to question society's goals and decide that those goals are not worth having.

Merton used the concepts of cultural goals and institutionalised means to classify various *types* of deviance, as shown in the table below. So, for example, if you adapt to the cultural structure by accepting both the goals and the means, you are a *conformist* (you do not deviate). On the other hand, if you accept society's goals, but reject the methods of achieving them, you could *innovate* with new methods (which may then be deviant or criminal).

Table 1: Individual adaptations to the cultural structure

		Goal	Means
1	Conformity	+	+
2	Innovation	+	−
3	Ritualism	−	+
4	Retreatism	−	−
5	Rebellion	+/−	+/−

+ you accept the goal or means
− you reject the goal or means

In Table 1, then:
- *Conformity* is when you accept both the goals and the means that are available to you to achieve those goals.
- *Innovation* occurs when you want the goal, but use alternative or illegitimate means of achieving it.
- *Ritualism* occurs when you continue to conform to society's standards, even though you have lost sight of the goal.
- *Retreatists* reject both the goal and the way in which society says you should pursue it.
- *Rebellion* occurs when you oppose the accepted goals and means, but you formulate new goals and means.

Let us look at an example: your goal is to own the latest fashions, and look rich. The means to achieve this is by making money. But, you lack experience and qualifications to get a well-paid job, or you can only get poorly paid jobs that will never pay enough for you to achieve the goal.

If your behaviour is:
- *Conformist*: You want the clothes and will earn the money in a legitimate way. You might get a job in a shop and work extra hours to earn more to buy that new pair of jeans.

- *Innovator*: You want the clothes, but refuse to accept the bad jobs. You will use alternative means of getting money. You work on the black market making cash, sell drugs, or shoplift the clothes you want.
- *Ritualistic*: You will be fixated by the means to the goal, even though the goal has gone. You will work hard very dutifully, but will never go out and buy anything. You tell yourself you never wanted fancy clothes anyway. You just carry on working and saving and working.
- *Retreatist*: You will just say 'forget it', and reject both the fashion and the job to earn the money. You might refuse to make money, refusing to work in a 'normal' job or to wear any sort of fashionable clothes. You become a dropout, and live on the street.
- *Rebellion*: You reject the fashion and the money making. You establish a new set of goals for yourself. Instead of the latest fashion being your goal, you might want happiness or adventure, or social justice. You might join a revolutionary terrorist organisation.

As indicated, for Merton, your place within the social structure is an important factor in your response to social strain. He was especially interested to analyse why certain categories of people in society have higher rates of deviance than others. For Merton, members of the working class are more likely both to share society's dominant goals and to find those goals frustrated. In consequence, it is to be expected that working-class members are most likely to choose innovative and deviant means of satisfying their goals. This does not mean that poverty in itself results in deviance, according to Merton. It is the combination of poverty and the acceptance of the cultural goal of wealth that creates the problem.

By contrast, among members of the lower middle classes, where norms to conform to mainstream social values are stronger, there is a greater likelihood that people will resort to ritualism. In this position we find junior bureaucrats and clerks who place enormous importance on respectability, and on sticking to the rules.

Critique

Merton's analysis is problematic in a number of ways. Firstly, he tends to assume that once a deviant, always a deviant. Yet it appears that people often participate for a while in deviance and then change their behaviour later in life, as we shall see.

Secondly, Merton's theory does not explain why those who have easy access to the goals of the society become deviant. The theory explains why the poor and those on the edge of the society will become deviant and commit violent acts, but the wealthy also commit crime and use violence.

Thirdly, Merton appears to explain deviance in individualistic terms.

> Merton's theory does not explain why those who have easy access to the goals of the society become deviant.

The various responses that he discusses seem to derive from personal decisions without further influence from social values. We shall see how other functionalist theories attempt to respond to these problems.

Fourthly, Marxists criticise Merton for missing a basic point in his analysis of America. According to them it is the capitalist nature of American society that creates the problems referred to by Merton.

Finally, perhaps the major criticism of Merton is that he, like other functionalists, assumes that members of society necessarily share the same values and norms. In the following section it will be showed how Marxists differ from this conception. Non-Marxist sociologists have also been critical of the idea of value consensus. They argue that modern societies are characterised by the existence of subcultural groups with values that differ from, or are in conflict with, the dominant values of society. In this view deviance indicates the existence of *subcultural values* and not an inability to live up to the shared values as Merton argues.

Despite these criticisms, Merton's ideas are still very influential in theories of crime and deviance.

Marxism

Marxists believe that society is based upon the power struggle between ruling and working classes who form conflicting interest groups, and the criminal justice system reflects this conflict. The task for researchers then is to understand how the criminal justice system is constructed, whose interests are protected, and who is excluded and vulnerable. **Karl Marx** (1818–1883) argued that capitalist societies are based upon the exploitation of those without economic power. Those with economic power (the ruling class or bourgeoisie) are able to promote and protect their economic interests in all aspects of the society. The laws in a society are a reflection of these interests and operate to protect the bourgeoisie's interests against the interests of the powerless.

Marxists see society as being in a constant state of conflict (unlike Functionalists). As a result there is no 'shared value system', or universal 'moral order', but only that imposed by the ruling elite. This is done through either force or the threat of force (which only works in the short term), or by cultural means (ideology). A successful ideology makes people believe that the ruling class's value system is the right way to live. The criminal justice system operates to create social order, protect private property (a fundamental aspect of capitalism) and protect those who have wealth from those who do not. Through socialisation, economic and social inequality is seen as 'normal'; any political or social protest against it will be viewed as 'extreme', 'dangerous' and deviant. The social and economic group you belong to will determine how you are treated by the criminal justice system, and whether or not your interests and behaviours are protected.

The above emphasis on law and the criminal justice system, however, does not imply that Marxists do not attempt to explain why people commit crime. Here is a sample of these attempts. In these theories the structure of capitalist societies is emphasised as the main contributing factor to crime.

The *classic Marxist theory of crime* is that proposed by the Dutch criminologist Willem Bonger. Bonger argued that the capitalist emphasis on private ownership of the means of production and the profit motive engenders egotistic tendencies (Bonger, 1916). People become competitive, greedy and selfish. All classes develop these value orientations and therefore crime will always be high in capitalist societies. The solution Bonger proposed for this situation was to replace capitalism with a socialist system. As was the case with many Marxists, Bonger predicted that in the socialist system, where the means of production would be held in common, the egotistical tendencies characteristic of capitalism would be replaced by altruistic tendencies and the crime rate would drop.

Bonger's ideas initially had little influence in criminology due to the lack of interest in Marxism among scholars. Marxist themes, however, surfaced again in the 1970s in so-called *neo-Marxist theories*. Another example of this continuing tradition is the synthesis of Marxism and symbolic interactionism in the book, *The New Criminology*, by the British scholars Ian Taylor, Paul Walton, and Jock Young (Taylor et. al. 1973) – also referred to as radical criminology. This book is mainly a critique of existing theories of crime and deviance and ends with a general outline of the authors' views concerning the requirements of 'a fully social theory of deviance'. In these works capitalism remains the main cause of crime.

A new emphasis was the link drawn between the class struggle in capitalist societies and crime. The *political* nature of crime was thus emphasised. This included 'crimes of resistance' by the working classes that are attempts to rebel against capitalism. For Marxists, working-class criminals often played the role of Robin Hoods stealing from the rich and redistributing this wealth to the poor. Capitalists, on the other hand, try to protect their interests by 'crimes of domination and repression' like corporate crime and crimes by the government. (We will elaborate on this in the section on corporate crime.)

Critique

An important criticism of neo-Marxist theories came from a group of scholars who named themselves *New Left Realists* as distinct from neo-Marxists (whom they renamed Left Idealists). These scholars included

Jock Young (a former neo-Marxist), John Lea, Roger Mathews and Richard Kinsey (Mathews, 1987; Young, 1987; Young and Mathews, 1992; Young 1994). Although critical of neo-Marxists' ideas as being too 'idealistic,' these scholars still view themselves as socialists and try to develop a 'realistic' alternative to Left Idealism. Based on evidence from victimisation surveys they are critical of attempts to deny the high crime rates in working-class areas and among certain minority groups. They also see the Robin Hood image of working-class criminals as too romantic. Victimisation data show that in reality working-class areas experience a major crime problem and working-class criminals often victimise other members of the working class. They do not see the solution to the crime problem as the overthrow of capitalism, but rather in changes within capitalism in line with socialist principles.

But how do Left Realists explain crime? The following three concepts are major features in their explanations:

1   *Relative deprivation*: Left Realists reject the idea that *absolute* deprivation (e.g. poverty, unemployment) necessarily results in crime, as many poor and unemployed persons do not commit crime. To them it is *relative* deprivation that is the important factor. This refers to a *feeling* of being less well off that develops when people compare themselves with other individuals or groups that are better off, or when they compare themselves with a certain standard of behaviour (e.g. material success) and see that they do not reach this standard. Relative deprivation is accompanied by feelings of unfairness and injustice that make people turn to crime to rectify the position. Importantly *all* sections of the population can experience relative deprivation, not only the poor. You can be enormously wealthy but still feel deprived compared to even wealthier people and revert to crime to appease your feelings of deprivation. According to Left Realists, the media contribute to relative deprivation in modern societies through the emphasis on economic success and high lifestyles.

2   *Subculture*: People in a similar situation of relative deprivation can collectively try to solve their problems by forming a subculture. This does not imply that it has to be in the form of a criminal subculture, however. One other alternative to crime is religious subcultures that emphasise moral values opposed to criminality.

3   *Marginalisation*: Individuals develop feelings of marginalisation when they feel that society and government do not attend to their problems – they are socially and politically shifted to the margins of society. This typically occurs among groups who are not organised to protect their interests and even may lack clear goals. This lack of organisation (e.g. labour unions) may result in the use of violence and rioting to express feelings of frustration.

Symbolic interactionism

The term *symbolic interactionism* was introduced into sociology by Herbert Blumer (Blumer, 1969). There are five principles of interactionism which are of interest for our purposes. Firstly, interactionists base their ideas about social action on the view of human beings as active, thinking actors. Put negatively, they *deny that human behaviour is determined* by biological drives, social structure and cultural factors. Social actors are not puppets. Instead, these factors merely form the framework in which action takes place without determining the action.

Secondly, humans have the capacity for symbolisation. This implies that we interpret or give meaning to our surroundings. Language (as a system of symbols) plays an important role in this process. The world around us, both the world of material objects and the social world, has no intrinsic or inherent meaning. One person may see a snake as an evil spirit, another may see it as a poisonous reptile and another as a tasty meal. Interactionists commonly refer to this process as defining the situation or the social construction of reality. The important implication of this view is that we can only fully understand social action by taking into consideration the perspective of the actor.

Thirdly, humans also define themselves. It is a matter of huge importance how I define my own identity, whether I see myself as a child or a parent, a student or a lecturer, whether I see myself as powerful or weak, as a success or a failure, attractive or ugly, male or female, and of course law-abiding or deviant.

Fourthly, to understand social action we have to study the specific situations in which action takes place – we have to link the action to the contextual factors that influence action. Who are the people involved? How do they define their situation? How does the interaction between people influence their definition of the situation? What role do cultural, social, structural and other environmental factors play in the interaction? In the light of this complexity interactionists emphasise that one *cannot fully predict the outcome of interaction.*

Finally, interactionists work with a *processual* view of reality. Interaction is seen as a process that unfolds over time. In this process people define the situation and are influenced by each other as well as by social structure and culture. They make choices in the light of these influences. They may reproduce existing social and cultural patterns, but they may also change these patterns. Interactionists use the concepts 'natural history' and 'career' to emphasise the ongoing and evolving nature of action.

Symbolic interactionism and deviance

What are the implications of these views for the study of crime and deviance? At this point we will examine three major contributions by interactionism to understanding crime and deviance. Firstly, we look at interactionism's insistence on the relative nature of deviance and crime, i.e. the fact that definitions shift from society to society. Secondly, we look at interactionism's focus on how deviants themselves define their actions by way of justifications and excuses. And thirdly, we examine probably interactionism's most influential contribution to criminological theory, namely labelling theory.

Earlier on in our discussion of the definition of deviance and crime we indicated that sociologists commonly view deviance as relative (not intrinsic to behaviour). It is in large part interactionists who have been responsible for propagating this viewpoint. In this view, behaviour only becomes deviant or criminal if defined or interpreted as such by specific people in specific situations. In other words, deviance and crime are socially constructed. Like Marxists, interactionists are also interested in the processes in which social norms and labels are developed and applied. They also emphasise the point made by Marxists that power plays a big role during this process.

But interactionists are critical of functionalist and Marxist explanations of crime and deviance as they view these explanations as being too *deterministic*. In their emphasis on structural strain and capitalism these approaches do not explain *why not all* people experiencing strain or not all members of the working class commit crime.

The definition of the situation: The deviant's perspective

Interactionism's second major contribution has been to highlight the manner in which deviants explain their deviance. In this context interactionists distinguish between justifications and excuses (Scott and Lyman, 1968). *Justifications* refer to explanations of deviant behaviour in which the deviant accepts responsibility for the behaviour but rejects the negative connotation of the behaviour. *Excuses*, on the other hand, refer to explanations of deviant behaviour in which the deviant admits that the deviant behaviour is bad or wrong, but does not accept full responsibility for the behaviour. Sykes and Matza (1957) elaborate on this with their idea of *techniques of neutralisation*. They argue that deviants are often aware that their behaviour is unacceptable and therefore experience feelings of shame and guilt. Deviance will continue, however, if deviants can neutralise these feelings. It is in this context that techniques of neutralisation play a role. These are ways in which individuals deny responsibil-

> In this view, behaviour only becomes deviant or criminal if defined or interpreted as such by specific people in specific situations.

ity for their actions (para. 1 below – an excuse), or deny that what they did was wrong (paras 2–5 – justfications).

1 *Denial of responsibility:* It was not my fault; someone or something else made me do it. (I was drunk so it was not really my fault.)

2 *Denial of the victim:* The victim in some way deserved what happened, so the act was not wrong. (He insulted me first so he deserved to be hit. She was wearing sexy clothes, so she was asking to be raped.)

3 *Denial of injury:* The act is acknowledged, but the harm to the victim is denied. (The company is wealthy, so stealing from them does not hurt them. She enjoys being called names; it does not hurt her.)

4 *Condemnation of the condemnors:* The act is acknowledged, but justified as 'everyone does it', or blamed on those who criticise. (I know cheating in sociology essays is wrong, but everyone was doing it. Anyway, the course is just too hard. See how corrupt the police and politicians are.)

5 *Appeal to higher loyalties:* Here the person tries to use a moral stand to justify their action, and say that they were justified in their actions. (My friend was being robbed, I had to shoot the thief, and anyone else would do the same.)

Labelling theory

The third major contribution by interactionists is known as labelling theory. Their main interest is not to explain why people deviate as such, but to explain why some people define themselves as deviant (develop a deviant identity or self-concept) and become involved in deviance on a continuing basis. Although early conceptions of the labelling process are present in Frank Tannenbaum's book *Crime and the community* (1938), it is only later that it was developed more fully by writers such as Edwin Lemert, with a book entitled *Social pathology*, published in 1951 and Howard Becker, with his 1963 book entitled *Outsiders: studies in the sociology of deviance*.

Lemert makes the important distinction between primary and secondary deviance (or 'deviation' as he referred to it). *Primary* deviance refers to situations where individuals violate social norms, but do not view themselves as deviant. This kind of deviance has no implications for the social roles they fulfil. *Secondary* deviance, on the other hand, refers to situations where individuals accept deviant identities and organise their lives around deviant roles. What interests interactionists is the process through which individuals move from primary to secondary deviance. In explaining this process they emphasise the effects of *negative reactions by the public* on primary deviance. (Labelling theory is

> Their main interest is not to explain why people deviate as such, but to explain why some people define themselves as deviant.

Being labelled a deviant may result in a *self-fulfilling prophecy*, i.e. where a label makes its own reality happen.

sometimes referred to as societal reaction theory.)According to interactionists, when the public reacts negatively to primary deviance it is often in the form of *labelling* – the person who breaks the rules is for example labelled as 'drug addict' or 'whore'. These labels carry negative *meanings* and the labelled person is thus publicly stigmatised.

The label may also become what Becker referred to as a 'master status'. By this he meant that in their reaction to deviants, the public tend to forget about other statuses that the individual may have (e.g. father, teacher, soccer player) and only concentrate on the deviant (stigmatised) status (e.g. 'drug addict').

Something similar happened in South Africa under apartheid. Race became the ultimate label. Not only did your skin colour influence how others interpreted your behaviour, but also predetermined where you could live, eat, swim, work, play sport, marry and also influenced what would happen if you committed a crime. In the criminal justice system labelling played a large part in determining how you were treated. Whether or not you were arrested, charged and convicted depended to a large degree upon your skin colour.

Although interactionists at first emphasised the role of powerful official agents of social control (police, courts, prisons) in the labelling process, they later also took the role of informal labelling (e.g. friends, family) and even self-labelling into account.

But what are the effects of being labelled as deviant in public? According to interactionists one major effect is on the labelled individual's self-concept. Interactionist theory emphasises that our self-concepts are greatly influenced by the reactions of the people with whom we interact. Being labelled a deviant may result in a *self-fulfilling prophecy*, i.e. where a label makes its own reality happen. The labelled individual then defines him/herself as deviant and acts as a deviant. The deviant may then also be isolated by family and friends. According to Becker the deviant career from primary to secondary deviance is completed when individuals become part of a deviant subculture due to the changes in self-concept, social isolation and lack of economic opportunities.

Young's (1971) discussion of police reactions to marijuana smokers illustrates the above arguments. During the 1960s and 1970s marijuana smokers were labelled 'pot-smokers' and were treated negatively by the police. As a result they felt different, isolated and rejected, and formed organised communities that not only lived separately, but contained a range of social and income-earning activities. Marijuana smoking now became central to their social lives. At a following stage, some of these young people were arrested or spent time in jail. That heightened their sense of estrangement and resentment against society, and made it more difficult for them to earn money to support their lifestyles. After all, they now had 'criminal records'. Over time, within these communities a deviant subculture formed which justified and rationalised the use of marijuana, and built up negative prejudices against the rest of society that also reinforced their deviant self-concepts.

When labelling theory became popularised, it was viewed as a radical theory. At that time the accepted view was that social control deters deviants from further deviance. What the labelling theorists in effect were saying was that official control causes deviance! The concept *deviance amplification* coined by Wilkins (1964) became widely accepted to refer to this phenomenon where control activities that are intended to curtail deviance in actual fact lead to an increase in deviance. This has important implications for how society reacts to deviants. We may well bring about what we hope to stop.

> There is the danger that individuals will be seen as puppets who passively accept what other people say about them.

Critique

Becker does show the power of others, and, in particular, the role of authority, in the creation of crime. However, the theory does have weaknesses. If deviance is only caused by the acting out of a label, it implies that the individual is not responsible for his or her actions. If this is the case, it follows that we should not punish people, as they are not to blame for their own actions, and that sounds wrong. There is the danger that individuals will be seen as puppets who passively accept what other people say about them. In many formulations of labelling theory there is a tendency to explain the labelling process in this rather deterministic fashion as if deviants *automatically* accept the label of deviant.

This, of course, contradicts one of the basic principles of interactionism that emphasises individual choice and agency. Rogers and Buffalo (1974) show in an interesting article how deviants actually have a number of ways in which they can fight back when labelled. For example, they can reinterpret the label ('terrorist' becomes 'freedom fighter') or they can offer justifications and excuses for their deviant behaviour.

Summary

This chapter has introduced some of the basic concepts and theories in the study of crime. We started with the notions of deviance and crime, and emphasised that definitions of crime and deviance are always linked to specific societies. There is no universal and absolute notion of what constitutes a crime. Then we took a first and preliminary look at how one explains the origins of crime. There are three broad categories of theory: functionalist, Marxist, and interactionist. Each one has a different take on how societies operate, and how they hang together. In consequence, they have very different notions of where crime comes from. The table below summarises the main principles and criticisms of the three theories.

Table 2: Main principles and criticisms of sociological theories of deviance

	Functionalism	Marxism	Interactionism
What is society?	Based on shared values and goals, and the contribution of parts to the whole.	Based on conflict between ruling class and working class. The criminal justice system protects the interests of the ruling class. Capitalism causes greed and selfishness.	Based on individual interaction through symbolic communication.
Causes of deviance	For Durkheim, when social norms do not sufficiently regulate individual behaviour. For Merton, when the available means are inadequate to achieve social goals.	When working class individuals rebel against the capitalist system. For Left Realists, relative deprivation, anti-mainstream subcultures, and marginalisation.	When actions are defined or 'labelled' as deviant. The labelling act itself aggravates the process of becoming deviant.
Main criticisms	There is no value consensus in society.	Working class crime is not politically inspired.	Deviants are not passive recipients of labels.

From this consideration of basic concepts and theories, we turn now to the first issue of importance, that of violence.

Websites

These are general sites that will provide you with specific information. Remember that they will not all agree on the causes, rates or consequences of deviance and crime. If a website does not work, search for it or other information on www.google.com or www.lycos.com

South African Police: www.saps.org.za
Medical Research Council: www.mrc.ac.za
Interpol: www.interpol.int
USA Bureau of Justice: www.ojp.usdoj.gov
United Nations Crime and Justice Information Network:
www.uncjin.org/index

2 · Deadly deeds: violence in South Africa

Suicide and rape: two examples of violent crime. In this chapter we examine Durkheim's understanding of suicide, and feminism's understanding of rape.

'Residents of an East Rand squatter camp each paid R22 to bail a man accused of murder out of prison. Then they killed him.' (Sunday Times, 4 July 1999)

A couple argues about the husband's drinking, and he attacks her. She does not want to report the attack as it might make him hit her again.

A girl goes out drinking with friends. She gets drunk and her boyfriend rapes her. She does not know what to do. She wants to report it to the police, but she is frightened that no one will believe her, that she will be seen as causing the rape. She doesn't want her parents to know she had gone out. So she does nothing, stays at home, scared of her boyfriend, and all other men.

Introduction

In this chapter we look more closely at violent deviance and crime. South Africa is a very violent nation, with one of the highest rates of murder and rape in the world. This violence affects us all either directly (you might have been a victim of violence yourself), or indirectly (you alter your behaviour to reduce your chances of becoming a victim, you avoid certain places at night, you install security in your house). Why is South Africa so violent, and how can we make it safer?

When we read of crimes in the newspapers, the ones that usually get the most attention are those acts of violence, usually extreme violence, such as murder, rape, or violent robberies, that are unusual or involve important people. If we relied only on what the media told us, we would

Some violent acts are not criminal or even deviant.

come to the conclusion that crimes of violence are complex, often between strangers, and involve planning on the part of the aggressor. However, the evidence points to the contrary. Most violent crime occurs in the home, between people who know or are related to each other. The causes are often minor.

Some violent acts are not criminal or even deviant. When a government uses capital punishment it is not called murder. If a soldier in a war kills an enemy soldier, he is not accused of murder. What is the difference between two men fighting in a boxing ring and the same men fighting in a bar?

In this chapter we examine two groups of theories of violent crime and deviance. The first group are functionalist. We start with Durkheim's seminal theory of suicide and show how he uses that to understand society as a whole. The second group, feminist theories, are used here to analyse rape. Feminists believe that all of society, including the criminal justice system, is male dominated and biased against women and that this oppressive structure supports the crime of rape. They believe that only through massive social change and the empowerment of women can violence against women be reduced.

Definitions of violence

Violence can range from verbal intimidation to the killing of someone. It does not have to be a physical attack to be violent. The most extreme form of violence is homicide, which is the killing of a person. The term *homicide* is quite a wide one. It includes suicide, the killing of oneself, justifiable homicide (the legitimate killing of another – e.g. killing another soldier in war), culpable homicide (the killing of another person, usually accidental such as in a car accident) and murder (the wilful killing of another). Remember that all these definitions of homicide are socially constructed – there is nothing absolute about them. For instance, some people believe that abortion is a form of murder. Others believe that when the government uses the death penalty it is murder. For every country the definitions of these acts are constructed by the lawmakers. Generally, however, the killing of another person is seen as a criminal act.

Researching violence is difficult because of the different definitions that can be used for the act, and the problems of interviewing victims. Not everyone will view a certain act as 'violent', and not all violent acts will be reported to the police. Violence between friends, family and relatives is reported less often than violence between strangers, even though most violence is between people who know one another. Women who are attacked or raped by their husbands or boyfriends are also less willing to report the matter. They might fear further attacks, or think that they will not be taken seriously by the police. Finally, it is impossible to interview dead victims of violence.

Homicide

South Africa has one of the highest homicide rates in the world. Every day between 20 and 30 people are killed, and many more severely injured. Why does this happen? Why do people want to kill other people? Are murderers evil, like in movies or books, or just normal people? We have to turn to theory to try to find out.

Table 3: International homicide rates for the year 2000 (per 100 000 people)

Country	Homicide rate	Country	Homicide rate
Columbia	80	Ukraine	11.3
South Africa	55	USA	9.4
Russia	26.5	Argentina	4.4
Brazil	19	UK	1.3
Latvia	18.2	Japan	0.6
Mexico	17.2		

Suicide

Suicide is the taking of one's own life. We often think of suicide as an intensely personal act; someone being weighed down by accidental tragedy in love or in financial affairs. If this were true, suicide rates would vary quite randomly between countries, groups, genders or age, but they do not. This can be illustrated by the findings of an analysis of South African suicide rates for 2001 by the Medical Research Council (Matzopoulos, 2002). In line with international patterns, South African men have a higher suicide rate than women – for every one suicide by a woman, five men commit suicide. Suicides among women peak in the 15–19 age category while for men it is in the 25–29 category. The choice of method of suicide also differs among women and men. While poisoning is most common among women (35,6% of women chose this method), men tended to favour hanging and firearms (77,8% of the cases fell in these two categories).

As is the case in other countries, the suicide rates of population groups differ in South Africa. Suicide is proportionally most common among whites, followed by Asians and coloureds. Blacks have the lowest rate. To be specific: Although whites make up 9,6% of the population of South Africa, they are responsible for 30,1% of suicides. Asians consti-

Emile Durkheim, being a macrostructural functionalist, wanted to show that society has an overwhelming influence on the way individuals act.

tute 2,5% of the population and commit 5,3% of suicides. In the case of coloureds, the suicide rate is roughly in line with the proportion they make up of the population (8,9% of population and 8,4% of suicides), while the black proportion of suicides (56,6%) is much lower than the proportion they make up of the population (79%). Another noticeable feature of the white suicide pattern is that it peaks at a higher age compared to other groups (49,7% of the cases fall in the 30–49 age range). There is also a noticeably high rate among whites in the 65+ age category. Regarding methods used, whites favoured firearms (45%) while Asians (54,5%), blacks (54,7%) and coloureds (35,4) favoured hanging.

It is patterns like the above that stimulated Durkheim to attempt the first major sociological analysis of suicide rates.

Durkheim

In his famous book, *Suicide* (1897), Emile Durkheim, being a macrostructural functionalist, wanted to show that society has an overwhelming influence on the way individuals act. A dramatic way to do that, he thought, would be to examine suicide, which then, as now, was seen as a highly personal act in response to some random incident. In examining suicide rates in Europe at the end of the nineteenth century, however, he found constant differences between countries, regions and more particularly between religions. For example, quite curiously, Protestants seemed to commit suicide more often than Catholics. What was it about religious beliefs that could make this happen?

Durkheim suggested that there were two important factors that influenced suicide: the *level of integration* (that is how well people fit into the community) and the level of regulation (how much they are controlled by it). Durkheim proposed that we all need some level of integration and regulation in our lives, but when our experience of them is either too great or too small we are driven to deviant and self-destructive acts. That led him to deduce that there were four types of suicide, as shown in the table below.

Table 4: Types of suicide

	Too little	Too much
Integration	Egoistic	Altruistic
Regulation	Anomic	Fatalistic

Let us examine each of these in more detail.
- **Egoistic suicide** occurs when the individual is not well integrated into social groups. Durkheim based his conception of this type of suicide on various statistical trends. He found that Protestants had a

higher suicide rate than Catholics and Jews. For Durkheim, a higher level of individualism among Protestants causes them to break away from established religion more often. On the other hand, married people (especially if they have children) have significantly lower suicide rates compared to the unmarried. Also, suicide rates are lower in times of political strife when people tend to work together for a common goal. Durkheim's basic principle is thus that problems arise when individuals have no social support in the form of family or community. They have nobody except themselves to live for – they are all on their own, and if anything goes wrong, they feel the full weight of the catastrophe, and so suicide results.

Durkheim's basic principle is thus that problems arise when individuals have no social support in the form of family or community.

- **Altruistic suicide** occurs in situations of very high integration into society. Here individuals believe that the community they live in is more important than their own lives. These conceptions are often related to religious or political principles. Examples would be the Japanese Kamikaze pilots of WWII who crashed their planes into US ships, killing themselves for their country, or modern Palestinian or Tamil suicide bombers. They give their lives for the sake of a bigger cause.

- **Anomic suicide** occurs when there is too little normative regulation of individuals. To Durkheim it was important that society regulates individual desires as people may develop aspirations that they cannot achieve. For example, suicide rates rise during an economic depression. In Durkheim's view individuals who experience such a decline in their living standard should learn to accommodate their new (lower) position in society. It is under such conditions that individuals find it meaningless and often extremely difficult to continue living. *(Does this sound familiar? Remember the earlier reference to Durkheim's influence on Merton's theory?)*

- **Fatalistic suicide** will occur when you are overly regulated, if you have no control over what you do and how you do it. Imagine that you are in a prison that controls every minute of your day. You have no control over what you wear, eat, read, see, etc. Your life feels overwhelmed by someone else's power. You have utterly no say in your own life, and so you commit suicide.

Earlier we noted that Durkheim is a functionalist. Why is this so in his treatment of suicide? Mainly because (i) society is seen as more influential than the individual; and (ii) values and norms are what hold society together – when there is a disintegration of this value consensus, society begins to fragment and individuals start to suffer. (See also the first book in this series, *What is Sociology?*, for a more detailed treatment of Durkheim and his contribution to functionalism.)

Critique

As we might expect, even though his work on suicide was groundbreaking, Durkheim's work did not go uncriticised. Most of the critiques have, also predictably, come from interactionists.

The interactionist Jack Douglas (1967) criticised Durkheim for putting meanings to people's behaviour that cannot be tested. How can we measure the subjective experience of levels of integration and regulation, by merely analysing statistical trends? Durkheim gives us no method to test if they are 'too much' or 'too little', or even what a 'normal' level should be.

Douglas argues further that official statistics should not be taken at face value. Official suicide statistics are constructed by officials. Doctors, police and coroners label certain acts as suicides, and their particular attitudes and beliefs will be influential in this process. For instance, among Catholics suicide is a terrible sin and doctors might not want to say that death was a suicide in order to lessen the pain felt by the victim's family.

In spite of the criticisms, Durkheim was able to analyse an important social behaviour and apply scientific research methods to its study. He showed that individual behaviour is influenced by the social structure in which we live – we do not make 'individual' choices, but rather operate within a social framework that influences our choices. Deviance will occur when individuals are in an environment where they have no sense of belonging or identity. The point to underline here is that Durkheim was able to show that a supposedly personal and intimate act was deeply influenced by the structure of broader society.

Interactionism and suicide

We now turn to an overview of attempts by interactionists to address some the issues that they raised in their criticism of Durkheim. According to interactionists, suicide should be analysed as a situated action with attention to the meaning that individuals ascribe to their suicidal behaviour. How can researchers overcome the problem of ascribing their own meanings to someone else's suicide act? Well, they use of a variety of sources, such as interviews with suicide survivors and analysis of suicide notes and diaries.

The most comprehensive study from this perspective is that by Baechler (1979). In his study Baechler distinguishes four main types of suicide, indicating different kinds of meaning for the suicide act. Thus, **escapist** suicide refers to situations where the individual wants to escape from something. This may be where a situation has become intolerable; or a case of *self-punishment* where the suicide is an attempt to atone for a real or imagined fault. **Aggressive** suicide is an attempt to harm somebody else through, for example, *vengeance* with the aim of making other people feeling guilty (killing yourself when your husband/wife wants to divorce you), or through *blackmail* (e.g. a child who commits suicide if the parents refuse him/her permission to do something). **Oblative** suicide (literally, meaning *offering*) can be self-sacrifice as with suicide bombers in a political struggle, or an attempt to attain a higher state of unity with a god. Finally there is **ludic** suicide (literally, playing a game) like Russian roulette or risking one's life to prove a point.

Rape

While at first glance the concept 'rape' seems straightforward, this is not the case. Not only do different criminal jurisdictions define rape differently, but members of the public also do not always agree on what precisely rape entails. In some countries the rape of a wife by her husband is not considered a crime, but a normal part of the marriage. (Only as recently as 1983 did this law change in South Africa.) In terms of current South African criminal law, for example, men cannot be raped. Oral rape and rape with objects are also excluded from the South African legal definition. The position in South Africa may change in the near future as the Sexual Offences Amendment Bill that is currently before Parliament proposes certain changes. If promulgated, the definition of rape will be broadened to include homosexual rape. Although penetration by objects other than genitals and forced oral sex will be sexual offences, they will not be classified as rape.

South Africa has one of the highest levels of reported rape in the world at 121 per 100 000 (SAPS data for 2001). But there are some doubts as to the accuracy of figure. It is a crime that has a low level of reporting to the police. Surveys show that women are not willing to report rape for a variety of reasons: fear of reprisal by the rapist (often a family member), shame, fear of being labelled responsible for the rape, or fear of and lack of faith in the police. It is estimated that only one in ten rape cases is reported to the police. Of those, under 20% will result in a conviction of the rapist. The procedure to report a rape is intimidating and often the victim is seen as being at fault herself for 'encouraging' the act by dressing in a certain way or being alone, or in a bar, or by acting in a particular way.

The South African Medical Research Council reported in 2002 that 85% of all rapes reported involved girls between ten and 14 years old. A third of rapes were by teachers, 10% by boyfriends and 21% by relatives or strangers. Men will generally rape women of the same socio-economic and racial group, and some child rapists appear to believe that raping a virgin will cure AIDS.

Feminist theory

Before we launch into feminist theory it is worth remembering that there are a fair number of different feminist theories. There are, at the very least, radical feminism, Marxist feminism, liberal feminism and Black feminism. While not all feminist theories therefore have the Marxist focus on class analysis, feminists, like Marxists, focus on the *power struggle* between *conflicting interest groups* in society (in this case women and men). Like Marxism, feminism can therefore be classified as an example of the broad category of *conflict theories*. While the issue of violence against women is perhaps most prominent in the work of radical feminists, this issue is important to all feminists.

In the 1970s feminists challenged existing notions of rape, rapists, and rape victims (Chasteen, 2001). Feminists argue that rape has to be understood as being a result of a male-dominated society and male aggression. Male domination is accepted as the 'norm', and the oppression of women through law, economy, education and violence is upheld and unquestioned by the majority of the society. Against this background feminists argue that *rape is a crime of violence, domination and control, not sex. Any woman can be a rape victim, any man can be a rapist, and rape occurs in many forms, including date rape and marital rape.*

Feminists emphasise the *lack of consent* by the woman as a key element in rape, rather than the behaviour of women or the sex drive of males. They reject the idea that women encourage men by the way they dress or act, and that they might even secretly enjoy being raped. This view has now become the popular slogan 'No means no' in feminist discourse.

Feminists argue that the 'common sense' view that rape is caused by the sex drive of only a small group of males is also false. Instead, they say that any man can be a rapist. To support this view, attention is drawn to the fact that rapists are often known to the woman raped – often an acquaintance or even a boyfriend and husband. Rapists are therefore found in all strata of society. They share the desire to dominate and control women through violence as a result of their socialisation into the culture of a male-dominated society. Brownmiller (1975), for example, argues that society is biased against women. It treats them as property, and rape is viewed as violation of property, not of a person. The rape of an unmarried virgin is seen as more serious than that of a married or a single sexually active woman, because the woman is more 'valuable' as a virgin! Think of marriage ceremonies and how the bride is passed from the 'ownership' of the father to that of the groom.

These types of attitudes, say feminists, also have an influence in the aftermath of rape. The police, courts and media are male dominated and discriminate against women both openly and more subtly. How many rape victims would like to be questioned and physically examined by a male police officer? Would they be believed if their attacker is a family member, boyfriend, or schoolteacher? In the courts, male judges have not always been sympathetic to the victims: a British judge in the 1970s declared that rape was impossible since in his view it was impossible to 'thread a moving needle'. A South African judge in 2002 said that a five-year old girl had enticed her adult rapist, and was thus to blame for her rape. A male-dominated society allows men to engage in rape, and makes women unwilling to report it. The social pressures not to report rape are high. The victim will fear being labelled as causing the rape in some way, or might fear further attacks. In some cultures it is very important that a girl remains a virgin until marriage, so she would be unwilling to report a rape.

Women need to be taught to be more sensible in their actions, says Paglia, to reduce their chances of being victims.

Critique

The above feminist arguments have not come away unscathed – even by fellow feminists. Their critics have called them unrealistic. Camilla Paglia (1992) argues that rape is a fact of life, and that her fellow feminists' arguments that the whole world can be 're-educated' are foolish. Would you go into a high crime area at night carrying lots of money? Women need to be taught to be more sensible in their actions, says Paglia, to reduce their chances of being victims, and not expect to be able to wear what they want and do what they want without consequences.

The idea that rape is a crime of violence, domination and control, and not sex, has also been challenged. In an overview of these arguments Goode (1997: 288) indicates that while rape *per definition* is always a crime of violence, at the level of *motivation* there are different ways in which rape can be sex in addition to being violence. For example 'for some men violence and sex are fused; for many men, rape is instrumental in gaining access to otherwise unattainable women; and finally, for some men rape is a sexual adventure'.

For the feminist Ann Cahill (2001) robbery is also a crime of violence, but the meaning of being raped differs from that of being robbed! While the motive for rape is therefore not always domination and control, it should be kept in mind that domination and control may be an *unintended consequence* of rape. The mere fact that some women are raped, by its threat, affects even those women who have not been raped. Women have to be more careful about where they go at night, how they dress and with whom they go out. But the threat still remains, even in the home.

The feminist reinterpretation of rape in the context of a male-dominated patriarchal society is an important correction on previous interpretations of rape. In the past, the victim was blamed or rapists were seen as an exclusive group of sexual deviants. However, that created the impression that rape is culturally justified in most societies. This is hard to believe as probably the majority of men, despite being in a powerful position in society, would view rape as unacceptable. In this regard feminists reflect elements of the functionalist view of the existence of a value consensus in society.

Against this background many scholars argue that rape should be seen in the context of certain subcultural groups in society. Consider Martin and Hummer's (1989) research on date rape at university campuses in the United States of America. The research clearly shows the existence of extreme sexist attitudes in fraternities where women are viewed as commodities – women are deliberately used by members. They are used as sexual bait to attract new members, to serve men at social gatherings, and also as sexual prey. In addition, the use of violence and physical force is widely accepted. Alcohol use is an integral part of the subculture and is widely used to obtain sexual access to women – many of whom are raped while under the influence of alcohol.

But what about other theoretical perspectives on rape? The following are brief comments on interactionist interpretations of rape.

Interactionism

Sociologists Scully and Marolla (1984) analysed interviews with convicted, incarcerated rapists to gain some insight into the subjective perspectives of rapists. Many of the rapists denied that their behaviour amounted to rape and *justified* their actions by presenting the victim as blameworthy. They argued that women are seductresses, women mean 'yes' when they say 'no', most women eventually relax and enjoy it, and that nice girls don't get raped. Some of the rapists admitted that their actions were morally wrong and without justification. But they made *excuses* for their behaviour by appealing to influences outside their control – for example, the influence of alcohol, drugs and emotional problems.

It is important to note that the above interpretations of rape from the perspectives of interactionism do not replace the basic feminist argument about rape. Many of the justifications of rape used by rapists reflect cultural stereotypes of women. We could say that feminist interpretations focus on the macro socio-cultural context of rape, while the interactionist perspectives provide insight into the micro interaction situation where rape occurs.

Summary

We have seen that acts of violence are greatly influenced by the wider society whether, following Durkheim, they arise from a lack of regulation and integration, or, following the feminists, from social beliefs about male domination. Both of these would accord in one way or another with functionalist theory. For functionalists, the broad values and norms of society have a powerful influence on individuals. Crime thus occurs either because the normative binding of society has been fragmented, or because individuals see crime as the right thing to do. Functionalists see crime therefore partly as the result of social disorder, and the role of the criminal justice system as restoring that order. However, remember that functionalists also see crime itself and efforts at prevention as useful in confirming and strengthening social values against crime.

Radical feminists view society as male-dominated. For them, rape is a result of this domination. For feminists, rape is an act of power, not sex. The criminal justice system is biased against women, protecting male interests and making violence against women an easy crime to commit and get away with. Unlike functionalists, therefore, they see the existing structure of society as part of the problem.

We turn now to the matter of juvenile delinquency.

Functionalists see crime therefore partly as the result of social disorder, and the role of the criminal justice system as restoring that order.

Websites

Federal Bureau of Investigation: www.fbi.gov
Rape Crisis: www.rapecrisis.org.za
USA Rape Abuse and Incest National Network: www.rainn.org
UK Rape Crisis Federation: www.rapecrisis.co.uk

3   Having fun or committing crime: juvenile delinquency

An overwhelming proportion of crime is committed by young men in the age group 17–20. Here we investigate three main factors in explaining this phenomenon: social control, subculture and gangs.

Lucy is 17. She likes to go out drinking and partying with friends at clubs. When she gets drunk, she often breaks glasses and makes a lot of noise, but no one complains because she is a good customer and is wealthy.

Mike also likes to go out drinking with his friends. They cannot afford to go to clubs, so they hang out on the street and drink. He has been arrested several times for drinking in public and disturbing the peace. His criminal record will mean that he will have difficulty in getting a job, so instead he will spend his time on the street with his friends, drinking.

Introduction

Let us start with the bald statement that most crime is committed by young men. There are two broad kinds of explanation for this. Society exercises less control over young people of particular ages; and young people often belong to deviant subcultures and to gangs. In addition to that, society makes young men different to young women. Let us see how these 'bald' statements look when you spell them out in more detail.

Two of the most persistent findings in criminology are that (i) young people commit proportionately more crimes than other age groups, and (ii) males commit proportionately more crimes than females. In general, the crime rate tends to rise in the early teens and peak in the late teens or early twenties – with the rate of females peaking at an earlier age (Muncie, 1999). The following are some of the patterns in South Africa (Schönteich, 1999):

- In 1995/96 the conviction rate per 100 000 of the population (all offences) of males in the 18–20 age category was 2 283 in comparison with 318 for males in the 7–17 age category and 1 481 for males above 20 years of age. The corresponding rates for females were 277 in the 18–20 age category, 37 in the 7–17 category and 205 in the above 20 category.
- In 1999 almost 43% of persons awaiting trial were between 18 and 25 years old, while this age group only comprised about 20% of the population.
- The only national victimisation survey conducted in South Africa, in 1997, found that young people are disproportionately likely to be victims of crime. Of the victims of at least one violent crime, 31,5% were in the 16–25 age category, while 30,1% of victims of non-violent crime were in the 26–35 age category.

Most crime is committed by young men.

It is statistics like these that have resulted in a concern about so-called juvenile crime internationally. Older generations have probably always been concerned about the 'deviant' behaviour of young people, but it was only during the 19th century, with the development of industrial capitalism and rapid urbanisation in Europe and North America, that juvenile delinquency attracted special attention (Muncie, 1999). This concern was related to middle-class concerns about the increase in the urban working-class population who lived in poverty and reverted to crime to make a living.

It was also during this era that the practice of separating juvenile offenders from adult offenders originated. Philanthropists deemed it inhuman for juvenile offenders to be treated like adults. They also worried that contact with adult offenders would result in reinforcing criminal tendencies among juveniles.

South Africa followed these trends under British influence. The current position in South Africa is that a juvenile offender is a person between the ages of seven and 17 years. (Persons below the age of seven years are not deemed to have criminal capacity and can therefore not be convicted of a crime.) Separate institutions for the handling of juvenile offenders like reformatories have also been established following the British and American examples. We should note, however, that the proposed Child Justice Act currently going through the parliamentary process proposes that the age of criminal capacity be raised to ten years, and that in the case of children who are between ten and 14 years of age the court will have to prove that the child has criminal capacity.

Explaining delinquency

Delinquency and the age structure of society

Why is there a sudden rise in delinquency rates in the early teenage years, and why does the rate decline from the late teens? One of the most comprehensive attempts to answer this question is by David Greenberg (1977). He argues from a Marxist perspective that in modern industrial societies children of all classes share a common relationship to the means of production, that is, they are excluded, due to compulsory schooling and exclusion from the labour market. This has produced an extended period of childhood compared to previous centuries when children started to work and married earlier. Modern children, then, are 'in limbo' much longer. Delinquency is influenced in various ways by this social position of children. During the teen years, there is great emphasis on consumer goods (e.g. fashionable clothes, CDs, eating out) among teenagers. In the absence of sufficient money, teenagers 'innovate' to achieve their goals (remember Merton?). Theft rates decline in the later teens because many teenagers leave school and obtain legitimate positions in the labour market.

Greenberg furthermore argues that it is especially those teenagers who do not excel at school who resent school most and revert to delinquency to express their resentment. Schools are also status systems because teachers evaluate and rank learners. The self-esteem of many learners is negatively affected in this process and expressed in delinquent behaviour.

Greenberg also found that the violence rate for males peaked later compared to other forms of delinquency. He links this to the problems created for working-class males who do not find employment. These males experience masculine status anxiety that is then expressed in violent behaviour.

To fully explain the decline in delinquency rates in the later teen years Greenberg incorporated aspects of the *control perspective* in his interpretation. He argued that getting involved in conventional institutions like employment and marriage controls deviant behaviour. Some comments on this theoretical perspective are thus called for.

The control perspective

The control perspective rests on the assumption that deviance is always a possibility and unless individuals are controlled, deviance will occur. The theoretical question is thus: Why don't all people deviate? And not: Why do people deviate? – as is the case in other theoretical perspectives.

Control theories have various theoretical roots. Some go back to

Durkheim's notions of regulation and integration. Others originate with *rational choice theories*. In this view humans calculate the benefits and costs (e.g. punishment) involved in deviance and if the benefits outweigh the costs, they will use deviant means to obtain their goals.

For Hirsch, strong social bonds stop youth from committing crime.

Perhaps the best-known theory of delinquency in the control perspective is Travis Hirschi's (1969) *social bond theory*. Hirschi argues that there are four bonds that bind individuals to the social order: (i) *Attachment* pertains to the emotional links that juveniles have to conventional others like their parents, school and teachers. If juveniles have positive relations with these agents they will deviate less because it would be too shameful to disappoint the agents, (ii) *Commitment*: if juveniles are committed to conventional aspirations, e.g. educational and occupational goals, they will rationally avoid deviance not to endanger their aspirations, (iii) *Involvement* refers to the time juveniles spend on conventional activities like homework and conventional leisure activities such as organised sport. The greater their involvement, the less time they will have to 'hang around with buddies' and the less the opportunity for deviance, (iv) *Beliefs:* If juveniles support conventional beliefs, such as respect for the law and police, this will also control their behaviour.

Does the above sound familiar? Hirschi's theory is perhaps closest to common sense conceptions about deviance. Chances are that your parents, teachers and community leaders have already lectured you in these terms. Hirschi's ideas have also generally been confirmed by research, but it is important to note that the statistical correlation between social bonds and delinquency that has been found in research is not very strong. The implication of this is that factors such as positive relations with family and the school, and conventional beliefs do limit delinquency, but are not the only or most important factors that influence involvement in delinquency (Akers, 1999).

Delinquency, subterranean values and drift

Matza and Sykes (1961) start out by arguing that deviants are very similar to other people. For these writers, the value system of any society is complex and consists of competing values. Alongside the *dominant conventional values* (e.g. hard work), there are also *subterranean values* that are in competition with conventional values but are still accepted by many people. Examples are 'leisure values' such as adventure, excitement, and thrill-seeking as well as aggression and violence. These values are not intrinsically deviant but underlie the deviance of juveniles of all classes because juveniles express these values in inappropriate situations such as public drinking and rowdiness.

In his later book *Delinquency and Drift*, Matza (1964), influenced by interactionism, argues strongly that delinquents are not determined by society but rather *drift* according to choice between society's dominant values and subterranean values. People are not fixed into a deviant lifestyle. They later desist from delinquency because they have not been committed to these values in the first place. As they become adult with more responsibilities, they move away from subterranean values and into conventional ones. The fact that delinquents often use excuses and justifications for their actions, what we earlier called techniques of neutralisation, shows that they are strongly influenced by mainstream values, otherwise they would not need to deal with their shame and guilt in this way.

Critique

Sykes and Matza's ideas have not been accepted uncritically, however. They are, for example, rather vague about the specific conditions under which juveniles drift toward subterranean values and about the choice of living out values such as adventure and excitement in a delinquent rather than conventional manner.

Marxists and strain theorists would ask about the social factors that 'force' people into crime and keep them there, such as poverty and biased policing. They would say that Matza ignores large-scale social factors that influence the individual's ability to become deviant and non-deviant.

Furthermore, is it true to say that we all share the same set of values, even within the same society? Values and norms change quite clearly from the wealthy to the poor, from one religion to another, from one ethnic group to another, from one region to another.

In addition, it is not clear that all techniques of neutralisation are similar in leaving society's central values untouched, as Matza wishes to say. Saying that someone else made me do something that I know is 'wrong' is one thing. It does not challenge fundamental values in society. But, saying that we steal from the wealthy because they exploit us, is quite different. It questions the very basis for some quite central social values.

Delinquent gangs and subculture

In the analysis of juvenile delinquency, the terms *gangs* and *subculture* go together. The concept 'subculture' is often vague but has the general connotation of a group of (often young) people with values that differ from the dominant values of society.

Despite all the academic interest in gangs, there is no generally agreed-upon definition of gangs. For our purposes it is sufficient to note that broadly speaking 'gangs' indicates crime that is committed in group context. This may be in the form of small groups of juveniles that opportunistically break the law, neighbourhood-based groups (so-called street-corner gangs), or highly organised crime syndicates. Regarding juvenile gangs, the focus has often been on street-corner gangs. This term was popularised by American sociologists who were interested in neighbourhood gangs that often 'hung around' on street corners.

The sociological analysis of the formation of these street-corner gangs has been strongly influenced by two theoretical perspectives, namely Merton's version of strain theory, and the subculture perspective. Subculture theorists are critical of the functionalist idea of value consensus. They argue that modern societies are internally differentiated and that not all people subscribe to the dominant values of society. While many of the theories that attempt to explain delinquent gangs integrate strain and subculture arguments, some reject the idea of strain and argue that a unique working-class culture exists. Subculture theories also differ from Merton in that they emphasise the group context of delinquency. Here are three of the most well-known theories.

Albert Cohen: Cultural deprivation and status frustration

In his theory, Albert Cohen (1955) adapted Merton's argument regarding structural strain and the inability to reach cultural goals. To Cohen the problem that arises for working-class males is that their goal to achieve *status* in conventional society is blocked. A major contributing factor in this process is that schools confer middle-class conceptions of acceptable behaviour like 'good manners', 'appropriate dress', and 'control of aggression'. Working-class learners, however, experience what Cohen refers to as *cultural deprivation* – they are not socialised into middle-class standards by their families. This cultural deprivation results in *status frustration* because teachers and peers look down on working-class learners. It is under these conditions that working-class males form gangs (subcultures) that *overturn* typical middle-class values and taunt members of the mainstream.

Cloward and Ohlin: Differential opportunity

Richard Cloward and Lloyd Ohlin (1961) start by accepting Merton's notion of *blocked legitimate opportunities* in the formation of delinquent working-class subcultures. But, they argue, to deviate individuals must also have access to *illegitimate* opportunities. Cloward and Ohlin then distinguish between three types of subcultures based on the type of illegitimate opportunities they provide. *Criminal subcultures* focus on criminal activities that produce an income like theft and robbery. These

A distinct culture
develops in lower-
class areas around
trouble, toughness,
or *smartness.*

gangs originate in working-class areas in which stable adult criminal patterns exist. *Conflict subcultures* originate in disorganised neighbourhoods where neighbourhoods gangs fight each other and status is conferred by fighting rather than income. The third type, *retreatist subcultures*, focuses on drugs and alcohol. These juveniles are 'double failures' according to Cloward and Ohlin, both in terms of conventional status criteria and in terms of being criminals or fighters.

Walter B. Miller: Lower-class culture

While the previous two theories combine aspects of strain and subculture, Walter B. Miller's (1958) theory is an example of a 'pure' subculture argument. For Miller, a distinct culture develops in lower-class areas around certain 'focal concerns' which directly contradict mainstream values, like *trouble* (achieving status through law-violating behaviour); *toughness* (proving masculinity through aggressive behaviour), or *smartness* (obtaining material goods and status by conning and outsmarting people rather than through hard work).

Subcultural arguments have drawn severe criticism. Research has shown that many people living in lower-class areas subscribe to the dominant middle-class values (Curran and Renzetti, 1994). To these writers, a criminal lifestyle is a rational reaction to a frustrating position in the social structure and not a different value system. It is actually the lower end of the lower class (the so-called underclass) that is most often involved in serious crime.

Youth gangs: USA and South Africa

Youth gangs in South Africa and the USA share many similarities. They are concentrated around large urban areas, are male dominated (although there has been a significant increase in female gangs in the USA) and are concentrated in economically deprived areas.

Much research has been conducted on gangs in the USA, and the information can be used in part to understand gangs in South Africa. Gangs in the USA range from small non-criminal groups, to the Gangster Disciples, with over 30 000 members in the Chicago area and estimated annual revenues of over $100 million from the drug trade. This is a very organised and highly structured group that in scale far exceeds the majority of gangs. The National Youth Gang Survey reported an estimated 26 000 gangs operating in the USA with over 840 000 members. Of these 60% are found in large urban areas. 50% are from the underclass, 35% percent working class, twelve percent middle class, and 3% upper class. 46% engage in selling drugs. Other common crimes are assault, theft and burglary. The gangs are mostly made up of minority ethnic groups – Asian, African-American and Hispanic – all of whom share similar economic and social stresses.

But what is the position in South Africa? The following are some important aspects highlighted in a recent overview of South African research (Kynoch, 1999):

Gangs predate apartheid and had already formed a part of urban living in cities in the early 20th century.

- Gangsterism is a major problem in black and coloured working-class urban residential areas in South Africa. While the rise of gangsterism is often linked to the apartheid system, historical evidence shows that gangs predate apartheid and had already formed a part of urban living in cities in the early 20th century. It is therefore more correct to see apartheid in the context of a long history of racial discrimination and the rise of industrial capitalism (accompanied by migration and urbanisation) in South Africa. This process resulted in a marginalised and poor urban population that was an important breeding ground for crime and gangsterism.
- Despite South Africa's official movement away from racism and discrimination in 1994, many of the socio-economic factors that initially contributed to the origin of gangs still persist. While the term 'youth gangs' correctly reflects the fact that many young males in working-class neighbourhoods join gangs, remember that both the high rate of unemployment and an ineffective welfare system keep older men in gangs too.
- One of the contributing factors to the persistence of gangs is the lack of effective policing. During the apartheid era police used gangs in the struggle against political rivals. Presently, corrupt police officials are themselves involved in the criminal activities of gangs or subvert the legal process by destroying evidence against gangs.
- Since the early 20th century affected communities have attempted to control the gang problem, but these efforts often resulted in the formation of vigilante groups that not only revert to illegal means to control the gangs but end up as gangs themselves.
- The importance of local community gangs has recently been overshadowed by the development of more organised gangs, often with links outside local communities – also with international syndicates. One aspect of this development is the importance of the international drug trade in South Africa when South Africa rejoined the global community after the democratic elections in 1994.
- Within the prison system a large-scale gang community exists – the so-called number gangs, e.g. 26s, 27s and 28s. New prisoners are recruited into the gangs, and are expected to continue their membership once they leave. Within the prison, gang membership offers the individual protection, sometimes a vital choice.

Gender and delinquency

Earlier on we saw that most crime is committed by young men. So far we have been concerned with examining the reasons why young people commit crime. But why is it mostly young men? Explaining that fact leads to two different kinds of question. The first, and this is the one which originally exercised the minds of criminologists, is, why do women commit less crime than men? The second, more recent, question is, why do men commit more crime than women, that is, what is it about men that is particular? Let us consider these two questions.

As indicated, when feminists initially approached this problem, they asked: Why do women commit less crime than men? In answering this question they often resorted to existing theories, like the control perspective. In the control approach, the striking aspect of women's behaviour is that they tend to be more conformist than men and subjected to more informal control measures relative to men (Heidensohn, 1996). And that in turn is a result of the patriarchal structure of society and the accompanying conceptions of femininity.

Approaching the gender ratio problem from the perspective of men, however, leads us to ask instead: Why do men commit more crime than women? This has led to an examination of conceptions of *masculinity* (Messerschmidt, 1993). This is interesting because it turns attention away from things like socio-economic factors that have dominated writing on this subject in the past. (Miller and his writing on the focal concerns of lower-class culture is an exception in this regard). Connell (1995) argues that various masculinities (multiple masculinities) exist in society and the task is to show how crime is influenced by these conceptions. He distinguishes between *hegemonic masculinity* (the dominant form in society at a particular time), *submissive masculinity* (e.g. homosexuality that has a lower status relative to hegemonic masculinity), and *marginalised masculinity* (variations of hegemonic masculinity found among working-class men, for example). We have seen that delinquent behaviour is often a compensation for frustrations in realising male status. It follows then that each of these masculinities will tend towards quite different behaviours.

Summary

In this chapter we have considered the phenomenon of juvenile delinquency from various perspectives illustrating the different levels of social reality, starting at the macro-level with values and structures and working down to the micro-level in situated interaction.

Table 5: Juvenile delinquency theories

Levels	Writers	Theoretical concepts
Values	Sykes and Matza, Hirschi	Subculture
Social structure	Marxists and feminists	Macro-level structural factors like stratification (class and gender inequality)
Situated interaction	Hirschi; Sykes and Matza; Cloward and Ohlin	Relationships with significant others (e.g. parents, teachers); illegal opportunities in crime

> Sociological theories are thus not necessarily mutually exclusive or competing perspectives.

- *Values:* The arguments about subculture, while critical of the functionalist idea of value consensus, retain the emphasis on the role of values in human behaviour; this emphasis is also found in the work of Sykes and Matza, as well as Hirschi's emphasis on beliefs.
- *Social structure:* Strain theorists, Marxists and feminists all emphasise the influence of macro-level structural factors like stratification (class and gender inequality) on crime.
- *Situated interaction:* Examples are the relationships with significant others (e.g. parents, teachers) highlighted by Hirschi; Sykes and Matza's emphasis on deviants' definition of the situation by means of techniques of neutralisation; and Cloward and Ohlin's contribution regarding the importance of illegal opportunities in crime.

A final thought: Consider the way in which sociologists integrate aspects of very different theoretical perspectives to explain crime, for example, Greenberg's integration of Marxist, strain and control perspectives. Sociological theories are thus not necessarily mutually exclusive or competing perspectives – in certain respects they highlight different aspects of social reality and it is up to scholars to see links and combine perspectives in an original manner to enable us to better understand human behaviour.

In this chapter much of the focus has mainly been on crime and deviance among the lower classes. In the next chapter we consider crime among the wealthier classes.

Websites

General links on USA gangs: www.coplink.com/gang1.htm
USA Office of Juvenile Justice and Delinquency Prevention
  ojjdp.ncjrs.org/resources/gangs.html
South Africa Centre for the Study of Violence and Reconciliation
  www.wits.ac.za/csvr/res/pubslist.htm

4 · Crime in suits: corporate crime

White-collar and corporate crime causes much more damage than that committed by the lower classes, yet it is less visible and much more difficult to pin down. Here we examine the social and cultural conditions which produce it.

A large company makes shoes. It sells them mostly in wealthy countries, but they are made in poor countries. The factories pay the workers very low wages. They have no union rights and the work is dangerous because of dust and chemicals. The company would not be able to operate these factories in its home country.

A company advertises its drink product as 'healthy', even though it contains only sugar, water and flavouring – should it be allowed to do so?

The World Health Organisation predicted that by 2020 around seven million people in Africa would die of smoking-related diseases per year. But tobacco cultivation is an important crop for many countries.

Introduction

Corporate crime forms part of a broad category of offences usually referred to as *'white-collar crime'*, the term popularised by Edwin Sutherland (1940) to refer to the offences committed by persons of 'respectability and high status' in the course of their occupations, as opposed to so-called 'street crimes', such as robbery and assault, more often associated with people of low status in society. The term is rather misleading as white-collar crime is strictly speaking not a legal category, but a catch-all term that includes both criminal and non-criminal offences. To complicate the issue further, the meaning of the term has been broadened to include all types of offences committed in organisations whether or not the offenders have a high status. Geis (1992) distinguishes between two categories of white-collar crimes, namely *occupational crime* (crimes committed by employees in organisations to benefit themselves) and *corporate crime* (crimes committed by employees of organisations to benefit the organisation). To explain more fully, corporate crime is crime that is committed by a company, organisation or even a government. It can include fraud, theft, making dangerous products, mislabelling products, lying to customers about the nature of the product, not providing goods or resources promised. It can also include the poisoning of people, destruction of the environment and death as a result of actions of the company. The companies or organisations themselves carry out these crimes. These crimes are often very complex and far more damaging than other crimes. They are also often not recognised as crimes by many people. The impact of corporate crime can only be guessed at.

> **Corporate crimes are often very complex and far more damaging than other crimes.**

In this chapter we examine both functionalist and Marxist theories in explaining corporate crime. As we have seen already, functionalist theories start from the assumption that societal values and norms influence people to commit crimes. These may be mainstream or subculture values.

Marxist theories, by contrast, focus on the nature of economic production, in general, and in this case, on capitalist production in particular. For Marxists, capitalism is a mode of production that encourages the ruling class to take advantage of the working class. The pressure to make ever higher levels of profit pushes business executives to take short cuts. Often the law is designed to favour these activities.

Corporate crimes: Case studies

Ellis Park soccer disaster

On 11 April 2001, 60 000 fans were in the Ellis Park stadium in Johannesburg with another 30 000 outside wanting to get in to see the match between Kaiser Chiefs and Orlando Pirates. A dangerous situation arose as more and more people tried to get into the stadium. Fences and gates were broken down as the crowd tried to gain access. Security staff fired tear gas at the crowd in an attempt to get them to disperse, but a stampede ensued. 43 people were killed and 250 injured.

The commission of inquiry into the disaster found that the security personnel were to blame for firing tear gas at the crowd, causing the stampede. The crowd was blamed for forcing their way into the stadium and for blocking the roads outside the stadium with cars with the result that ambulances could not get to the injured. The managers of the stadium were at fault for not having sufficient ticket booths for selling tickets, and not foreseeing that so many people would attend the match. The referees were criticised for not stopping the game immediately. Other factors that came to light were that very few tickets had been pre-sold, so many people arrived at the match hoping to get a ticket and see the game. The security guards lacked training to deal with the situation; a plan to deal with such a crisis was not in place.

Ten years previously a similar event occurred when 42 people were killed in a stampede when the same teams were playing at Orkney in the North-West Province. Apparently nothing had been learnt from the previous disaster.

Enron went bankrupt in 2002 after it emerged that the managers had been lying about the company's performance and profits for years.

Shell Oil and Nigeria

Nigeria relies heavily upon oil – around 80% of its export earnings come from this resource. Shell Oil operate oil wells in the Niger Delta region. The process earns the Nigerian government considerable foreign exchange, but also causes significant damage to the local environment. A protest movement by the Ogoni people of the Delta region led by Ken Saro-Wiwa called for action against Shell and the Nigerian government for the damage. Saro-Wiwa succeeded in mobilising local people against Shell, but was arrested by the military government. He was executed on 10 November 1995 in spite of the international outcry against the trial and sentence. Amnesty International and other international pressure groups raised questions about the legality of the trial, as well as the links between the Nigerian government and Shell Oil.

Enron

The Enron Corporation was one of the largest companies in the USA with annual revenues of US$100 billion (South Africa's total GDP in 2001 was US$136 billion) and employed 21 000 people in 40 countries. It went bankrupt in 2002 after it emerged that the managers had been lying about the company's performance and profits for years. They were able to do this with help from the accounting firm Arthur Andersen, who, instead of reporting accurately on Enron's performance, hid and destroyed evidence when an investigation started. Government tax officers had been bribed; Enron paid no tax from 1996 onward. Millions of dollars were given to political parties to influence the awarding of contracts. The bankruptcy meant that employees not only lost their jobs, but their investments and pensions as well. Thousands of investors lost all their money. Hundreds of other companies were affected, in turn directly causing individual financial and job losses.

Types of crime

Corporate crimes can be categorised into several key areas.

1 **Crimes against employees**

   This can take the form of paying employees less than they are worth, or not providing safe working conditions. 10 000 South Africans who worked for the asbestos company, Cape Plc, were diagnosed with diseases related to asbestos poisoning, diseases that will kill many of them. The company was also accused of using child labour.

2 **Crimes against customers**

   This entails making and selling goods that either do not work, are sold after their sell-by date, or are dangerous.

3 **Crimes against the public**

   Companies can affect the health of those outside the factory walls – pollution from factories affects the health of those who live nearby. The nuclear meltdown of the Chernobyl plant in the former USSR contaminated much of Western Europe. In June 2000 the oil tanker *MV Treasure* ran aground off the Cape coast. 1 100 tons of oil spilled from the ship, polluting large areas of penguin breeding grounds. In February 1994, at Virginia in the Free State, a mine slimes dam collapsed. It had not been built properly and had also been situated above a residential area. The mudslide crushed the suburb of Merriespruit, killing 17 and injuring 600. The company was fined R120 000.

4 **Crimes against the state**

   Companies can avoid taxation, or even corrupt the state. The controversy over the allocation of the arms contracts for the SADF in 2001, and the bribing of officials by several international corporations, showed the lengths to which some firms are willing to go to ensure they get the contract. Luxury cars at special prices were offered as bribes to senior officials to persuade them to support one company bid over the others.

Edwin Sutherland

As indicated, Sutherland (1949) was the first to call serious attention to white-collar crime as a significant area to study. He pointed out that those who were not poor, who had jobs, homes and good salaries, still committed crimes. He attacked the idea that crime was largely caused by poverty and the problems that come with it. Sutherland also demonstrated that this type of criminal act was far more damaging to the economy of the country than more visible crimes, and more harmful to the society itself.

Corporate crimes rarely make headline news, said Sutherland. And if they do, we do not remember them for long. There are six main reasons for this:

Corporate crime only becomes newsworthy when it occurs on a massive or unusual scale.

1 **Where is the victim?** Due to the apparent 'lack' of a victim, and the non-violent nature of the crime, corporate crime is seen by many as less serious than more visible crime, such as mugging. If a drug company gives free holidays to doctors to try to persuade them to promote their drug to patients, who are the victims?

2 **The crime is complex.** Often it is difficult to judge when a product becomes harmful. One needs specialised knowledge to understand when a crime is being committed with the global and highly complex nature of modern finance and accounting.

3 **Who is to blame?** Corporate crimes are rarely committed by a single person, but rather by a series of individuals, or by groups. For example, who do you blame if a car crashes because it is difficult to drive? The engineer who designed it, the workman who built it, the salesperson who sold it or the customer who drove and crashed it?

4 **Difficult to detect.** Crime on the streets is easy to see and recognise. A mugging is difficult to mistake for anything else. But corporate crime occurs out of the public eye, in company offices, and is often very similar to normal business practice. Companies will issue false reports on what they are doing and how well they are performing.

5 **Weak punishment.** If you kill someone and are caught, you will most likely end up in jail. If your factory is unsafe and a worker dies, you might be fined. Both actions result in a death, but result in very different punishments. Corporate crimes often result in lesser sentences than other crimes. Company executives have greater social standing, can afford better lawyers, and can pay large fines. Nike was able to manufacture its shoes in countries with dangerous working conditions and very low levels of pay. These acts would have been punishable in the USA, but because the manufacturing occurred outside that country, Nike could not be prosecuted for unfair labour practices.

6 **Little publicity.** Often, little public attention is given to corporate crime. The reasons for this lie in the explanations above. The issues are complex, often difficult to understand, and when there is no apparent victim, little media attention and often even less public attention is given to the stories. Corporate crime only becomes newsworthy when it occurs on a massive or unusual scale. The lack of attention helps to maintain the idea that corporate crime is not that great a threat, or that serious a crime to worry about. However, the impact of corporate crime can far outweigh the effect of more personal crimes.

Differential association

To explain both white-collar and street crime, Sutherland formulated a
general theory of crime. He suggested that 'a person becomes delinquent
because of an excess of definitions favourable to violation of the law over
definitions unfavourable to law violation' among one's associates
(Sutherland and Cressey, 1978: 78). Sutherland numbers among those
academics who at an early stage became critical of the functionalist
emphasis on value consensus. In opposition to this conception he argued
that modern societies are internally differentiated and that competing
sets of values exist. Sutherland used the term 'differential social organisation' in this regard. He was also influenced by interactionism, hence his
emphasis on the learning process in becoming a criminal. Much like subculture theories, Sutherland proposed that white-collar crime is strongly
influenced by the values and norms that corporate personnel associate
with, hence the name, differential association.

Differential association as a learning process that involves several processes:
1 *You learn the techniques of deviant behaviour, as with any social
   behaviour.*
2 *The behaviour is learned in close interaction with other people in small
   groups that you consider important.* You do not learn it from books,
   watching TV or listening to the radio, but from personal contact with
   others.
3 *When criminal behaviour is learnt, the learning includes the techniques
   and the specific set of motives, drives and attitudes that make the
   behaviour possible.* You have to learn the skills of crime, as you learn
   any other craft. In addition, people also learn how to motivate their
   behaviour. Remember Sykes and Matza's work on techniques of neutralisation in this context.
4 *The behaviour is altered by the definitions the individual holds of the
   law as being favourable or unfavourable.* If you see a law as
   favourable, or good, it is doubtful that you will break that law. On the
   other hand, if you and others around you are strongly critical of a law
   or of the government, it will be much easier to break the law.
5 *A person becomes delinquent because of an excess of definitions
   favourable to the violation of law over definitions unfavourable to the
   violation of law.* When most of the people around you hold opinions
   and beliefs that undermine the law, and the opposing views are very
   much in the minority, the chances are you will go with the majority
   view.
6 *Differential association may vary in frequency, duration, priority and*

intensity. How often you come into contact, the length of your contact, how early in your life you come into contact, and your attachment to, the source favouring law violation are all factors influencing the learning process.

7 *The process of learning criminal behaviour by association involves all the mechanisms that are involved in any other learning.* Criminal behaviour is learnt like any other behaviour.

8 *While criminal behaviour is an expression of general needs and values, those needs and values cannot explain it.* The desire to become rich or achieve status can explain both criminal and law-abiding behaviour. (From Sutherland and Cressey 1978, pp. 80–82.)

This is a powerful theory, and is very useful in understanding why corporate crime occurs. The person in a business will learn from others to 'bend the law' to make a few more rand. They might justify their actions and break more serious laws, and become even more corrupt. It is all a slow learning process.

<aside>
Critical theorists try to understand corporate crime as part of the wider set of business practices in capitalist society.
</aside>

Critique

Sutherland's work is very important and provided the first proper investigation of corporate and white-collar crime. However, the theories do not look at the structure of capitalist society and how it is designed to exploit the poor and powerless. The question to ask is, if a corrupt business culture exists to influence people entering the business world, how did it get there in the first place? On the other hand, there are some people who act individually, without, or despite, influence from their peers. Like the broader functionalist theory from which it derives, the theory of differential association tends to see individuals as puppets of societal forces.

Marxism/Critical theory

Critical theorists try to understand corporate crime as part of the wider set of business practices in capitalist society. Profit is the goal of capitalist organisations – it is how you are judged, and the means to achieve that goal are very wide and ever changing.

These theories are based upon a Marxist understanding of society, and are thus critical of modern capitalism and its effects upon society. Crime, say the Marxists, is a result of the wider social divisions in society. Those most at risk of being victims of crime are those who are also economically disadvantaged – the poor, women, children and those on the margins of society.

The rich and powerful commit crime as part of the continued process of capitalism, both national and global. They are also able to influence opinion away from their crimes and focus people's attention upon the crimes of the less powerful. It is no accident that when we think of criminals we tend to think of people from the lower classes. For Marxists, however, the poor and disadvantaged commit crimes because of their position in society. Their crimes are part of the struggle against the wider social and economic inequalities in the society. Crimes are the result of the wider social context, which is unequal and exploitative.

Capitalism is based upon the goal of achieving maximum profits. In an atmosphere of intense competition, with stakes worth billions of dollars, companies will be severely tempted to take short cuts. Often this pressure is increased by the influence of shareholders who invest their money in companies with the highest short-term profit.

Box (1983) argues that crimes of the powerful are more dangerous than those of the less powerful. What needs to be done is to expose these crimes and realise that corporations can kill, steal and maim, and often at a far greater rate than any individual could. He suggests that the corporate environment encourages people to take risks and go beyond the law to achieve their corporate goals. The boundaries that usually stop people from committing crime are lessened and the individual is more easily able to engage in crime.

For critical theorists the crimes of the powerful far outweigh the crimes of the rest. The acts of corrupt business people, government officials and others directly affect the rest of the population. They are also able to hide their activities, or cloak them as 'business' or 'state policy', but they are actually committing very serious crimes.

Critique

Marxists assume that corporate crime is directly linked to the capitalist economic system. The conclusion from this is that corporate crime does not occur in non-capitalist nations, but there is a great deal of evidence that crime occurs in all societies, no matter what their economic system.

Corporate crime in Africa

For Africa the problem of corporate crime is complex. First-World companies often manufacture products that are illegal to use in their own countries, but export them to the Third World. The large multinationals are able to influence national governments with the promise of financial investment and job creation, while local opposition parties often lack sufficient influence to halt the companies. In addition, the media in many countries are not free to report. Companies are able to engage in business practices that would be illegal in their home nations, in particular in areas of meagre wages, poor trade union representation and low work place safety and employee benefits. However, corporate crime is not caused only by foreign companies. Corruption and fraud occur within Africa on a wide and dangerous scale.

On an international level Africa does not fare well in terms of corruption. The organisation Transparency International rates countries around the world on a scale of 1 to 10 on their level of corruption (1 being most corrupt). The least corrupt nation is Finland (score of 9.9), the country with the lowest score is Nigeria (1.0), while South Africa has a score of 4.8. Nigeria is often seen as one of the most corrupt nations. Its former leader General Sani Abacha and his close family were able to loot the nation's wealth. It is estimated that he was able to steal over US$10 billion, of which US$3 billion was placed in foreign banks. In actions taken to attempt to retrieve the money, banks in Switzerland, the UK, France and elsewhere were asked to freeze his assets. Several major banks did not do so. Abacha was able to get so much money out of Nigeria because European banks allowed him to do so without asking questions, and by giving him accounts that could not be traced by police. Corruption does not happen in a vacuum, but requires the physical means to do it and the social environment to encourage and allow it to happen.

Corporate crime occurs throughout the world. In the poorer nations of the world, however, state corruption often harms the entire economy, leading to the decline of basic services, and even the deaths of its citizens. The crimes are often linked to the crushing of workers' rights and safety, poor pay, dangerous working conditions and lack of legal protection for the workers.

Corporations engaging in criminal activities are not only creating short-term harm, but also inviting others to do so. If the management of a company is seen to be corrupt by its employees, and escape punishment for their acts, then those employees will be encouraged to engage in corruption. Many officials in corrupt nations see corruption as a way of boosting their income. If they are not paid properly or on time, and their leaders are seen to be corrupt, these officials will be encouraged to make money by corruption, or take on other work. This will lead to the weakening of services, and corruption will become a normal activity.

In the poorer nations of the world, however, state corruption often harms the entire economy,

Summary

This chapter has concerned itself with the phenomenon of corporate crime. This kind of crime is often overlooked in spite of its effect upon society. We have examined two broad ways of understanding corporate crime. One is functionalism, and the other Marxism (or critical theory). Functionalists propose that we learn to be corrupt by absorbing the values and norms prevalent in the society, community or corporation in which we operate. In that sense, this is much like the subculture theories we looked at earlier.

For critical (Marxist) theorists, corporate crime is caused by the structure of capitalist society and its highly competitive pursuit of profit. For Marxists, the real criminals in capitalist society are not the lower classes who are usually targeted by the criminal justice system. They are, after all, simply struggling to survive and crime is merely one means of resisting an unjust system. The real criminals are the ruling class, who bias the criminal justice system to their own benefit. Ruling classes use their influence to hide the seriousness of corporate crime.

The question remains: How should we deal with these criminals? Will the threat of punishment stop companies from committing crimes? What kind of punishment would work? We will find some of these answers in the next chapter.

Websites

Amnesty International: human rights www.amnesty.org
Transparency International: State corruption www.transparency.org
Greenpeace – environment www.greenpeace.org
Sierra Club – environment www.sierraclub.org

5 Controlling crime: sociological theory and policy

And so, after all this, how does one control crime? Zero toler-ance, abolishing certain categories of crime and preventative measures are much in vogue these days. We look at why this is so.

Introduction

In this chapter we come to the point where we can expect to harvest some of the fruit of all our theoretical labours. Up to this point we have consid-ered how best to explain various acts of deviance. The next question is, then, how do those theories translate into practical action on the ground to lessen the incidence of crime? Put differently, how does explanation translate into practical policy? How do we go about the business of con-trolling crime?

But that question does not have a simple answer, for the reason that we are not the people who choose which policies to implement. Politicians and government bureaucrats make those decisions. And their approach to crime is often influenced by other things than pure theoreti-cal efficacy, such as political ideology. It matters a great deal whether those decision-makers follow, for example, conservative, liberal or social-ist ideologies. This is also the case in South Africa where the govern-ment's *National Crime Prevention Strategy* announced in 1996 is the first attempt in South African history to formulate a comprehensive policy to prevent and control crime.

In the discussion which follows, then, we start by considering briefly what conservative, liberal and socialist ideologies entail, and what the implications of these different ideologies are for policies of controlling crime.

Ideologies

Liberalism is an ideology that views individuals as essentially the same and inherently good, with the same dignity, and capable of restructuring society by means of their rational capacities. Liberals place great emphasis on individual freedom and individual rights to ensure that individuals are protected against arbitrary state power. Individual initiative is emphasised as opposed to reliance on the community and state.

Conservatism opposes many of the assumptions of liberalism and emphasises the importance of traditional moral values and institutions such as the family, church and community for social order. Conservatives believe that society is inherently differentiated and unequal, and they have a rather pessimistic view of human nature. This is especially true in respect of males who, in conservative eyes, are naturally violent, destructive and competitive. While conservatives are generally in favour of limited state interference in the lives of individuals, they argue that the state should protect moral values and traditional institutions if these, for example, are endangered by crime. Conservatives typically take a so-called *law and order* approach to the handling of crime.

Socialism is an ideological approach that is critical of the capitalist system associated with liberalism. In the form of social democracy associated with the welfare state, socialism has had considerable influence in western societies. Socialists favour: (i) *Egalitarianism:* that is, equality in community with others, as opposed to capitalist individualism that centres on self-interest and competition. (ii) *Moralism:* that is, values such as social justice, peace, co-operation and 'brotherhood' (sic) in contrast to capitalist exploitation. (iii) *Rationalism:* like liberals, socialists believe that social progress and individual happiness are possible to obtain through the application of human reason (Berki, 1975).

Policy and sociological theory

One way to divide up the multitude of sociological theories on crime and deviance is to say that each focuses mainly on one of three factors: values, social structure, and the individual. So, for example, in the functionalist tradition Merton emphasises the influence of the *values* of achieving wealth and status in society. Subculture theorists, likewise, would emphasise the influence of particular values found within specific groups. Marxists, by contrast, focus on unequal social *structures* as the root of crime. Finally, rationalist theories place importance on the *individual's* capacity for realistic decision-making in weighing up the options for or against crime.

> Conservatism emphasises the importance of traditional moral values and institutions such as the family, church and community for social order

Let us consider how the various ideologies approach these factors.

1 Values

While persons of all ideological persuasions would probably emphasise the importance of 'moral values' for social order, the exact content that they have in mind is very different. Conservatives, for instance, often argue that only a return to traditional religious values would solve the crime problem. In the light of their belief that societies are intrinsically unequal, they would furthermore argue that some people should lower their aspirations to live within their station in life and not aspire to become extremely wealthy. Liberals, for their part, argue for values such as respect for human dignity and respect for private property. Liberal feminists argue that violence against women will only be curtailed by changing conceptions of masculinity and femininity through public education. As indicated above, socialists emphasise values such as social justice, cooperation and brotherhood – values that will only be achieved by fundamental structural change to societal institutions.

> All ideological persuasions would probably emphasise the importance of 'moral values' for social order.

2 Social structure and social institutions

In this section we consider two important structural aspects of society, socio-economic change or capitalist development; and the underclass family.

Socio-economic change

For liberals the solution to crime lies mostly in capitalist economic development to create more employment opportunities and in general to create equal opportunities to 'level the playing fields'. Education and training are important aspects of this process. Within this approach it remains the responsibility of the individual to be self-reliant in the attempt to achieve a better position in society. In contrast to this, the socialist view is that capitalism causes crime and that the solution to the crime problem lies in the replacement of capitalism by a socialist/communist system where the means of production are held in common. In the light of the demise of communism in many East European countries in recent decades, this view has become less attractive. More moderate socialists favour a social democratic system that retains capitalism but tempers the inequalities by policies to alleviate poverty through full employment and extensive welfare provision by the state. This was the position in the so-called *welfare state* approach taken in many western counties roughly between 1950 and 1980.

A movement back towards liberalism has replaced welfare-ism since

the 1980s. Liberals criticise the welfare state for being hugely expensive
and for creating a 'culture of dependency' among the poor. The implication is that people do not take responsibility for their own lives, that to
some degree they view themselves as victims of their society, and that
there is not much they can do to better themselves.

Important for our discussion here is the fact that despite significant
rises in general welfare and standards of living in the 20th century, crime
has continued to increase in western societies. Resulting from this, conservatives argue that it is not increasing poverty that has caused a rise in
crime, but rather the development of a so-called *underclass*, with a dis-
tinctive family structure and value system.

The underclass family

In this view, the underclass is a group of people who are often unemployed, who come from broken families, are often involved in crime, but
most importantly have values that contradict those of mainstream society.
In particular, they have no inclination to work even when job opportunities are available, and they are quite content to live off welfare payments.

Members of the underclass, says Murray (1990), typically come from
families without fathers. That leads to a lack of discipline and application, a case of children 'running wild'. They are also often involved in
crime. The high incidence of crime in these communities leads to people
withdrawing from community life. As a result communities fragment, and
this makes it easier for crime to occur. Unemployed men, likewise, are
unable to support families, and this has consequences for their sense of
masculinity. At this point it becomes very tempting to resort to violent
crime to bolster damaged identities. All three these factors, then, interact
with each other, forming a particularly vicious circle of crime, unemployment and fragmented communities.

South Africa: welfare, neo-liberalism, and the underclass

What are the implications of these debates and viewpoints for South
Africa? It is generally assumed that one factor contributing to the high
crime rate in South Africa is the extremely high levels of poverty. We
could argue that with such levels of poverty, a welfare approach is in fact
needed in South Africa. Neo-liberals, however, would rely on economic
growth to provide employment as a solution. But in an overview of programmes in the USA to provide employment opportunities in high crime
communities, Bushway and Reuter (2002) conclude that over a number of
decades these programmes have not been effective in lowering crime rates.

3 Individuals, rehabilitation and punishment

The previous two factors discussed were on the macro-societal level. We now turn to attempts to control crime by focusing on the individual.

Rehabilitation is associated with liberalism's optimistic view of the capacities of individuals to be transformed.

Rehabilitation

Rehabilitation, in the sense of reforming criminals through treatment and re-education, has conventionally been associated with liberalism's optimistic view of the capacities of individuals to be transformed. In the social democratic welfare era of the 1950s and 1960s this was also the dominant approach toward handling juvenile delinquents. Individualised rehabilitation programmes presented by professionals, focusing on the needs of the individual, were the solution to criminal behaviour.

Despite the public's generally positive attitude toward rehabilitation, the academic attitude towards rehabilitation has been negative since the 1970s. This negativism is based on Martinson's (1974) conclusion that rehabilitation has little effect on recidivism rates of criminals (recidivism = return to crime after treatment). This conclusion resulted in a 'nothing works' attitude among academics and criminal justice officials. Many rehabilitation programmes were stopped. It is only recently that this negative view has been challenged by new research (Cullen, 2002).

This negativism had a major impact on the approach taken to the handling of criminals and delinquents in particular. If rehabilitation does not work or encroaches upon individual rights, it was argued, traditional criminal justice approaches should be used. *Punishment* rather than rehabilitation now became the preferred reaction to crime. In this context conservatives favour *deterrence* and *incapacitation*, while liberals re-affirmed the so-called *just deserts* model.

Punishment: just deserts and deterrence

The liberal emphasis on just deserts is based on the assumption that humans are rational beings and that if they offend, they must bear the consequences of their actions, i.e. receive their just deserts. The function of the criminal justice system is to dispense justice with the aim of retribution. While retribution is often associated with an 'eye for an eye' approach, this is not the focus in the *liberal justice* model. The focus is rather on *due process* and the *protection of the rights of the accused*. The punishment should be in proportion to the offence (just deserts). Rather than rehabilitation, the focus is now on the equitable and fair dispensing of justice.

While some conservatives also favour the just deserts model, closer to the heart of conservatism is *deterrence* as a function of the criminal justice system. Deterrence, like the control perspective, argues that, unless controlled, individuals will deviate. This is based on the assumptions that individuals are self-serving, and will rationally calculate the benefits and costs (punishment) of crime. If the costs outweigh the benefits, they will not choose crime. Conservatives thus view severe punishment in the form of fines or imprisonment as the main solution to the problem of crime. 'Prisons should not be five-star hotels', they say. Punishment should be an unpleasant experience to deter those punished *(specific deterrence)* and also send a message to the public that crime does not pay *(general deterrence)*.

Table 6: Political ideologies and policies for controlling crime

	Liberalism	Conservatism	Socialism
Values	Traditional religious values	Human dignity	Social justice, cooperation, brotherhood
Social structure	Employment, education	Underclass family	Socialism, welfare provisions
Individuals	Rehabilitation, due process, rights of the accused	Deterrence	

Recent trends in crime control

In the search for new alternatives for controlling crime, three approaches are currently in vogue: abolitionism and restorative justice, zero tolerance, and situational crime prevention. Let us consider each of these in turn.

Abolitionism and restorative justice

In this approach to crime control, the traditional emphasis in the criminal justice system on the role of the state, punishment and formal legal process is replaced by informal, and more communal forms of conflict resolution (Hughes, 2001:282). Like interactionists, *abolitionists* emphasise the relativity of crime – crime is not intrinsic to specific actions and action only becomes crime if defined as such by the state. In this approach, it is not necessary to view, for example, juveniles who vandalise property as criminals who should be dealt with in the criminal justice system. The vandalism should rather be defined as 'a problem' and 'trouble' and dealt with informally by the family or community. Abolitionists therefore are in favour of diminishing the role of the state and state institutions in crime control by decriminalising certain offences.

The arguments for abolitionism have also been linked to a different theory of justice, namely restorative justice. In contrast to the individualist approach of liberalism, restorative justice emphasises *communitarianism* – individuals as members of a group (Zehr, 1996). From this perspective, the liberal just-deserts approach is too formal, adversarial, and retributive (the establishment of guilt followed by punishment). Nor does it address the needs of the victim. Justice should aim to restore community relationships. This involves a process of *mediation* between the offender, victim, members of the community and state officials. In this process, the needs of the victim and offender are established together with the obligations of the offender to the victim and community. The outcome of the process is *reparation* of damage and providing *restitution* to the victim. Braithwaite's idea of *reintegrative shaming* entails that deviants should be shamed by the community but not stigmatised and socially rejected, as often is the case with labelling. Rather, the community should show forgiveness where the deviant shows repentance. Ultimately community relations are restored and the deviant is reintegrated into the community (Braithwaite, 1989).

> Justice should aim to restore community relationships.

This approach has produced a variety of *community-based* alternatives to the formal justice process such as victim-offender mediation, family group conferences (in which the problems associated with juvenile offending is handled in the family context, similar to reintegrative shaming), and educational programmes that have much in common with rehabilitation and treatment programmes. These programmes have been accepted across the ideological spectrum. Liberals and social democrats find some of the ideals of the welfare era and rehabilitation in the programmes attractive; the fact that the programmes can be more cost-effective than imprisonment appeals to neo-liberals; and the emphasis on community relationships is attractive to both socialists and conservatives. The Department of Correctional Services and the National Institute for Crime Prevention and the Rehabilitation of Offenders (NICRO) have increasingly implemented similar programmes in South Africa since 1992 (Muntingh, 1995).

Zero tolerance

'Zero tolerance' is a very popular term these days, but it is a very fuzzy one. Some people use it to mean 'getting tough' against crime. Others mean a specific *style of policing* based on an experiment with police foot patrols in Newark, USA. That experiment showed that there was less crime where police acted against minor public order offences (Sherman, 2002). A third group of people use the term to mean decreasing so-called incivilities (e.g. broken windows, refuse in the streets, public drunkenness), fear of crime among residents, and rising crime rates. They argue that if incivilities increase in a neighbourhood, residents will feel unsafe and withdraw from efforts to control disorderly conduct around them. This will encourage further incivilities, and result in a neighbourhood attracting criminals and spiralling into more serious crime. The now famous 'broken windows' thesis of Wilson and Kelling (1982) is often quoted in this context.

Zero tolerance supporters often quote the experience of New York City's dramatic success in lowering the crime rate during the 1990s. But the evidence for this success is not so clear. Greene (1999), for example, argues that there was a general decline in crime rates across the USA during the 1990s, not only in New York. Policing in New York during that time under the leadership of the chief of police, Bratton, included much more than acting against public order offences. Among other things, the entire police management system was changed and police intelligence gathering improved.

One drawback of zero tolerance policing is that it often results in an aggressive policing style that alienates members of the community. The approach furthermore presumes the availability of sufficient numbers of police officers. Further, while the approach may be effective to 'clean up' a specific area, the research evidence regarding the effect on the general crime level is rather skimpy at present.

Situational crime prevention

At a time when many crime control policies are seen as long-term affairs, or expensive and inefficient, situational crime prevention has gained popularity in recent times. In this approach crime is viewed as a 'normal' aspect of social life – something that we have to live with. Or to put it more formally, we should try to manage the risk involved in crime rather than try to solve the basic causes of crime.

This approach argues that the focus of crime control should be *preventative* (*before* crime takes place), and not *reactive, after* the deed has been committed. In this view it is possible to prevent crime by *limiting the opportunities for crime*. Protagonists argue that for crime to take place, there must be a potential offender, available victims, targets and an absence of control. There are three distinct strategies in limiting opportunities to commit crime: (i) *increasing the effort to commit crime* (e.g. steering locks on cars, fenced yards, ID badges), (ii) *increasing the risks to commit crime* (various forms of surveillance, e.g. burglar alarms, speed cameras, surveillance cameras, security guards, street lightning), and (iii) *reducing the reward of crime* (removable car radios, marking property) (Clarke, 1995).

During the 1980s neo-liberals favoured this approach. It implies that every individual can do something about crime. Neo-liberals are also in favour of it because it cuts down on state functions and puts more responsibility in the hands of the public. It is an approach much written about in South Africa at present. It has been widely implemented in public buildings (e.g. office buildings, shopping malls) and in the central business areas of cities (e.g. surveillance cameras).

Research results seem to support the effectiveness of this approach. It prevents crime from taking place or it increases the possibility of criminals being arrested. But there are problems. Where crime becomes more difficult in one area, criminals simply move to another, less protected area. Some people dislike the increasing surveillance in their lives and the growing 'fortress mentality' as people withdraw behind their fences and security devices (Crawford, 1998: 98–102). In addition, it is expensive, which means that some can afford it, and many, particularly those in high crime areas, cannot.

> Situational crime prevention implies that every individual can do something about crime.

Summary

So, crime control is not all plain sailing, and can be quite confusing. For the sake of clarity, it is important to keep three different aspects quite separate in your head. One concerns the consequences of sociological theories, the second concerns the conclusions from research evidence, and the third is the role of ideological factors in choosing between policy options. The uncertainty around crime control can arise from any or all of these aspects.

Websites

South Africa Department of Correctional Services: www.dcs.pwv.gov.za
USA Bureau of Prisons: www.bop.gov
California Prison Focus: www.prisons.org
Human Rights Watch: www.hrw.org
USA Community Policing: www.communitypolicing.org
London (UK) Metropolitan Police: www.met.police.uk
UK Home Office (police and prisons): www.policereform.gov.uk

6 Conclusion

At the end of our criminological journey, now, what do we do with this great array of theories? Theories can be our tools rather than our masters, opportunities rather than obstacles. The challenge is to be creative and playful.

In the course of this book we have discussed quite a range of theories. That could be confusing. In the table on page 60 we have pulled together all the theories discussed in the book and classified them according to the original division between functionalism, Marxism and symbolic interactionism. There are a number of things to note about this grand classification.

Firstly, you can see here how the three grand theories have multiplied into a variety of subtheories. So, for example, functionalism (starting from Durkheim) has produced a theory of suicide, strain theories (starting from Merton), and control theory. They all start from the principle that society's broad values and norms are profoundly influential in the way individuals behave.

Secondly, it should now be clear that while we have used particular theories for particular crimes, those theories can be applied in a number of different areas. Let us take the example of suicide. In Chapter 2 we analysed suicide with the help of Durkheim's functionalist theory. Here we showed how Durkheim used macrostructural factors concerning religious affiliation, marital status and place of residence to explain the incidence of suicide.

As we have seen, there has also been a great deal of work done on suicide by symbolic interactionists. These writers have focused on two specific areas: (i) the unreliability of suicide statistics; and (ii) the meaning of suicide to those committing the act. On suicide statistics, symbolic interactionists have argued that these numbers carry a false impression of truth. In effect, the process by which particular deaths are recorded as suicide, by for example coroners, is full of choices, interpretations and hidden meanings. On the meaning of suicide, symbolic interactionists show that the motives and intentions behind suicide can vary quite sharply, from escapist to aggressive motives.

It would be quite possible to imagine a Marxist theory of suicide, too (if there is not already such a study). Can you think what it might look like?

Thirdly, some theories do not fit into that neat three-way division. As we have seen, conflict theory and feminism appear to fall outside a neat classification. But there are different reasons for that. As we have indicated, feminism is actually an umbrella term for a range of theories. There are racial feminists, liberal feminists, Marxist and Black feminists. All of these to a greater or lesser degree see men and women as conflicting interest groups and emphasise the differences in power between the two groups. Conflict theory is related to Marxism because it sees society based on conflict, but it often draws a great deal from Weber in breaking away from the focus on economic class conflict. In short, some theories cannot be classified too cleanly – they have multiple roots in contrasting theories.

And, in a way, that is as it should be. Theories are not written in stone. They are not divine decrees. They are there to provoke us into asking new questions, seeing things in a new light, trying out new perspectives.

In the first book of this series, *What is Sociology?* (Graaff, 2001:24), we indicated that sociologists often work with more than one theory. Having more than one window to look through gives you a much wider and richer view.

Finally, having been through this variety of perspectives on crime, we can ask ourselves again, just as we did at the beginning of the book, is crime wrong? Should it be condemned absolutely? Here is a final thought concerning that question. It concerns the way that sociology, and here we mean macrosociology, looks at crime. The point is that your particular circumstances of life determine hugely how you behave. If you were born into a subculture that condoned violence, your chances of committing a violent crime would be much higher than otherwise. Sociologists learn to say very often, 'There, but for the grace of God, go I'. That could have been you or me committing crime, and going to jail.

> That could have been you or me committing crime, and going to jail.

Summary table of criminological theories

	Theory	Theorist	Main causes of crime
Functionalism	Strain theories	Durkheim Merton	• Lack of integration and regulation • Strain between goals and means
	Control theory	Hirschi	• Crime/deviance always a possibility; breakdown of social control; selfish human nature, rational calculation of costs and benefits of crime • Weak social bonds
Marxism		Marx	• Conflict between classes in society, capitalist control of media and criminal justice system
		Bonger, Box	• Capitalist desire for profit, competition, greed and selfishness
	Neo-Marxism	Taylor, Walton & Young	• Political nature of working-class crime
	Left Realist	Young, Lea, Mathews, Kinsey	• Relative deprivation, subculture, marginalisation
Subculture theories		Matza & Sykes	• Subterranean values contra mainstream; individuals drift in and out of crime
		Cohen, Cloward & Ohlin	• Gangs form subcultures contrary to mainstream culture (elements of strain theory)
		Miller	• Lower-class culture
		Murray	• Underclass values and family structure; fragmented communities (elements of control theory)
		Sutherland	• Learning deviant definitions and techniques (elements of interactionism)
Interactionism		Sykes & Matza	• Definition of situation: techniques of neutralisation (elements of control theory)
	Labelling theory	Lemert Becker	• Labelling of the actor, deviance amplification, self-fulfilling prophecy
Feminism		Brownmiller	• Male power with a desire to dominate women

Exercises

It has been an important concern of this book to present material in a way that constitutes a number of ongoing themes. The exercises here continue that concern for coherent argument. Social science is not about the recitation of hundreds of facts and figures. It is much more about the way that this material is ordered, argued, criticised and mobilised. And, if it were necessary, there is a great deal of educational theory to support that approach (Ramsden, 1992).

The exercises suggested below, then, come in different forms, some easier and some more difficult. The easier ones (let's call them **Level A** questions) typically ask you to do things like

- 'define' concepts
- 'explain what' writer X says about something
- 'summarise' what writer Y says about something else.

This is relatively easy because it asks you simply to understand what a writer is saying and to express it in your own words.

Slightly more difficult questions (**Level B** questions) will ask you to
- 'explain how' A links with B according to Marx or Parsons, or
- to 'compare and contrast' theory A and theory B, or
- to 'apply' theory X in a particular situation.

These questions take some extra thought because you are being asked to transpose ideas from one situation to another.

You may also be asked to
- 'construct a careful argument about …' In this case you are required to put together a coherent story which has logical and reasoned steps that follow from one another.

The most difficult, and the most interesting, questions (**Level C**) will ask you
- to 'construct your own examples' of a particular concept
- to 'discuss/critically evaluate' the ideas of, or the argument of, theory A, or
- 'do you agree with' this or that view.

These are more difficult because you have to start being creative and mobilise your own independent thoughts. They will also be somewhat longer questions because you will require further space to mobilise the steps of your argument. In the assessment of academic work, this skill is also considered the most valuable one.

Let us now consider some concrete examples from the material of this book.

Level A

1 Give brief definitions of the following terms, and where appropriate indicate which writer(s) uses them:

Anomie	Ritualism	Labelling	Rate of crime
Drift	Primary deviance	Strain	Strain
Subculture	Self-fulfilling prophecy	Integration	Conflict theory
Innovation	Subterranean values	Regulation	Techniques of neutralisation

2 According to Durkheim, how does the level of integration and regulation in a society affect suicide rates?
3 What is the difference between deviance and crime?
4 Why are corporate crimes rarely seen as being highly deviant?
5 How does the physical environment influence crime?
6 What is the difference between just deserts and deterrence in controlling crime?

Level B

1 Compare and contrast Sutherland and the critical theorists' views on corporate crime.
2 How does Merton's theory of anomie differ from Durkheim's? Which one is the more useful in explaining deviance in South Africa, do you think?
3 Compare and contrast Marxist and labelling theories in explaining why deviance and crime occurs.
4 How do symbolic interactionists and functionalists differ in how they see deviance occurring?
5 What does it mean to say that labelling causes an amplification of deviance? In your answer, explain the theoretical background principles of this statement.
6 What is wrong with functionalist theories of crime and deviance?

7 Distinguish the different types of gangs discussed in Chapter 3. Explain how they differ from one another.

8 Compare and contrast crime statistics from South Africa and the USA (you will need to go onto the websites of the SAPS and the FBI).

9 Both Sutherland on corporate crime, and Cohen, Cloward and Ohlin/Miller on gangs, use subculture theories. Compare and contrast these two sets of theories.

10 What is the difference between a theory of deviance and crime, and an ideology? Give examples of each and show how they are similar or different.

Level C

1 How well, do you think, can Matza's theory of drift be used to explain
   (a) corporate crime;
   (b) rape;
   (c) assault?

2 How does the community in which you live view crime? What crimes do they fear the most? What measures have been taken to reduce crime? To which approaches to controlling crime do these measures relate?

3 Do you agree with radical feminist views on rape? Give reasons. What do you think can be done to reduce the incidence of rape?

4 How do the media interpret deviance and crime? What theoretical perspective do they mostly use? Why? In your answer cite examples that you have seen on TV or read about in the print media.

5 Which do you think is the most useful theory in understanding the prevalence of gangs in South Africa? In your answer spell out the relevant principles of the theory and show how they are applicable to this case.

6 What measures can be taken, do you think, to reduce cheating in writing university assignments? In your answer, give examples of how cheating occurs, analyse the reasons why it happens, explain which theory/theories you are employing, and show how your suggested strategies could make a difference.

Annotated bibliography

The following is a selection of works that will be useful in any further study of crime and deviance in South Africa. This is only a limited list; you will find many more works in your library.

General texts
Becker, H.S. 1963: *The Outsiders.* MacMillan. London.
    A classic contribution to interactionist analysis of deviance.
Gelsthorpe, L. & Morris A. 1990: *Feminist Perspectives in Criminology.* Milton Keynes, O.U.P.
    A comprehensive work on the important feminist theories of crime and deviance.
Jupp, V. 1989: *Methods of Criminological Research.* Routledge, London.
    A tool-kit of research methods that will guide you in your work.
Muncie, J., McLaughlin, E. & Langan, M. 1996: *Criminological Perspectives.* Sage, London.
    Another good collection of criminology theory and practice.
Smith, M.D. & Zahn, M.A. (ed.) 1999: *Homicide.* Sage, London.
    An excellent book that covers the theory of homicide and reduction policies in the USA.
Sutherland, E. & Cressy, D. 1974: *Criminology.* Philadelphia, Lippincott.
    An older text, but very wide ranging and contains important original work.

South Africa
Bornman, E., Van Eeden, R. & Wentzel, M. 1998: *Violence in South Africa.* HSRC, Pretoria.
    A collection of works about violence in South Africa; a good source of in-depth analysis.
Marks, M. 2001: *Young Warriors.* WUP, Johannesburg.
    An in-depth, subjective study of youth in polical violence.
Shaw, M. 2002: *Crime and Policing in Post-Apartheid South Africa.* David Phillip, Cape Town.
    A very good book to use to obtain information on crime in South Africa.

Advanced readings
Cohen, S. 1985: *Visions of Social Control.* New York: Polity Press.
    An in-depth study of the theories and implications of social control and where it could go.
Garland, D. 1990: *Punishment and Modern Society.* Oxford, Clarendon.
    An important analysis of the role of punishment in the modern world.
Maguire, M., Morgan, R. & Reiner, R. 2002: *The Oxford Handbook of Criminology.* Oxford, Clarendon Press.
    A more advanced collection of the latest theories in criminology.

Bibliography

Akers, R.L. 1999: *Criminological Theories: Introduction and Evaluation* (2nd ed). Chicago: Fitzroy Dearborn Publishers.

Baechler, J. 1979: *Suicides.* New York: Basic Books, Inc.

Becker, H.S. 1963: *Outsiders: Studies in the Sociology of Deviance.* New York: Free Press.

Berki, R.N. 1975: *Socialism.* London: J.M. Dent and Sons Ltd.

Blumer, H. 1969: *Symbolic Interactionism.* Englewood Cliffs, N.J: Prentice-Hall.

Bonger, W. [1916]: *Criminality and Economic Conditions.* Abridged with an introduction by A.T. Turk. Bloomington: Indiana University Press, 1969.

Box, S. 1983: *Power, Crime and Mystification.* London: Tavistock.

Braithwaite, J. 1989: *Crime, Shame, and Reintegration.* Cambridge: Cambridge University Press.

Brownmiller, S. 1975: *Against Our Will: Men, Women, and Rape.* New York: Penguin Books.

Bushway S. and Reuter, P. 2002: 'Labor Markets and Crime.' In Wilson, J.Q. and Petersilia, J. (eds): *Crime: Public Policies for Crime Control.* Oakland, CA: Institute for Contemporary Studies.

Cahill, A.J. 2001: *Rethinking Rape.* Ithaca: Cornell University Press.

Chasteen, A.L. 2001: 'Constructing Rape: Feminism, Change, and Women's Everyday Understandings of Sexual Assault', *Sociological Spectrum,* 21:101-139.

Clarke, R.V. 1995: 'Situational Crime Prevention.' In Tonry, M. and Farrington, D.P. (eds): *Building a Safer Society: Strategic Approaches to Crime Prevention.* Crime and Justice: A Review of Research, Vol. 19. Chicago: University of Chicago Press.

Clinard, C. & Yeager, P. 1980: *Corporate Crime.* New York: Free Press; Toronto: Collier Macmillan.

Cloward, R. and Ohlin, L.E. 1960: *Delinquency and Opportunity.* Glencoe, IL: Free Press.

Cohen, A. 1955: *Delinquent Boys: The Subculture of the Gang.* New York: Free Press.

Cohen, R.W. 1995: *Masculinities.* Stanford, CA: Stanford University Press.

Crawford, A. 1998: *Crime Prevention and Community Safety: Politics, Policies, and Practices.* London: Longman.

Cullen F. T. 2002: 'Rehabilitation and Treatment Programs.' In Wilson, J.Q. and Petersilia, J. (eds): *Crime: Public Policies for Crime Control.* Oakland, CA: Institute for Contemporary Studies.

Curran, D.J. and Renzetti, C.M. 1994: *Theories of Crime.* Boston: Allyn & Bacon.

Douglas, J. 1967: *The Social Meanings of Suicide.* Princeton, N.J.: Princeton University Press.

Durkheim, E. [1897] 1951: *Suicide.* New York: The Free Press.

Geis, G. 1992: 'White-collar Crime. What is it?' In Schlegel, K. and Weisburd, D. (eds): *White-collar Crime Reconsidered.* Boston: Northeastern University Press.

Goode, E. 1997: *Deviant Behavior* (5th ed.). Upper Saddle River, N.J: Prentice-Hall, Inc.

Greenberg, D.F. 1977: 'Delinquency and the Age Structure of Society', Contemporary Crises, 1: 189-223.

Greene, J.A. 1999: 'Zero Tolerance: A Case Study of Police Policies and Practices in New York City', *Crime and Delinquency,* 25(2): 171-187.

Heidensohn, F. 1996: 'Gender and Crime.' In Maguire, M. et al. *The Oxford Handbook of Criminology.* Oxford: Clarendon Press.

Higgins, P.C. and Butler, R.R. 1982: *Understanding Deviance.* New York: McGraw-Hill Book Company.

Hirschi, T. 1969: *Causes of Delinquency.* Berkeley: University of California Press.

Hughes, G. 2001: 'The Competing Logics of Community Sanctions: Welfare, Rehabilitation, and Restorative Justice.' In McLaughlin, E. and Muncie, J.: *Controlling Crime.* London: Sage Publications.

Kynoch, G. 1999: 'From the Ninevites to the Hard Living Gang: Township Gangsters and Urban Violence in Twentieth-century South Africa', *African Studies,* 58(1): 55-85.

Lemert, E.M. 1951: *Social Pathology: A Systematic Approach to the Theory of Sociopathic Behavior.* New York: McGraw-Hill.

Martin, P.Y. and Hummer, R.A. 1989: 'Fraternities and Rape on Campus', *Gender and Society*, 3(4):457-473.

Martinson, R. 1974: 'What Works? – Questions and Answers About Prison Reform', *The Public Interest*, 35: 22-54.

Matthews, R. 1987: 'Taking Realist Criminology Seriously', *Contemporary Crises*, 11(4):371-401.

Matza, D. 1964: *Delinquency and Drift*. New York, Wiley.

Matza, D. and Sykes, G.M. 1961: 'Juvenile Delinquency and Subterranean Values', *American Sociological Review*, 26:712-719.

Matzopolous, R. 2002: *A Profile of Fatal Injuries in South Africa: Third Annual Report of the National Injury Mortality Surveillance System*. South African Medical Research Council and University of South Africa.

Merton, R.K. 1938: 'Social Structure and Anomie', *American Sociological Review*, 3: 672-682.

Merton, R.K. 1968: *Social Theory and Social Structure*. New York: Free Press.

Messerschmidt, J.W. 1993: *Masculinities and Crime*. Lanhan, MD: Rowman and Littlefeld.

Miller, W.B. 1958: 'Lower Class Culture as a Generating Milieu of Gang Delinquency', *Journal of Social Issues*, 14(3):5-19.

Muncie, J. 1999: *Youth and Crime: A Critical Introduction*. London: Sage Publications.

Muntingh, L. 1995: 'Introduction.' In *NICRO Research Series*, 2:4-5.

Murray, C. 1990: *The Emerging Underclass*. London: Institute of Economic Affairs.

Paglia, C. 1992: *Sex, Art and American Culture: Essays*. New York: Vintage Books.

Rogers, J.W. and Buffalo, M.D. 1974: 'Fighting Back: Nine Modes of Adaptation to a Deviant Label', *Social Problems*, 22:102-118.

Schönteich, M. 1999: 'The Dangers of Youth? Linking Offenders, Victims, and Age', *NEDCOR ISS Crime Index*, 5: 22-28.

Scott, M.B. and Lyman, S.M. 1968: 'Accounts', *American Sociological Review*, 33:46-62.

Scully, D. and Marolla, J. 1984: 'Convicted Rapists' Vocabulary of Motives: Excuses and Justifications', *Social Problems*, 31: 530-544.

Sherman, L. W. 2002: 'Fair and Effective Policing.' In Wilson, J.Q. and Petersilia, J. (eds): *Crime: Public Policies for Crime Control*. Oakland, CA: Institute for Contemporary Studies.

Steffensmeier, D.J and Terry, R. 1986: 'Institutional Sexism in the Underworld: A View From the Inside', *Sociological Inquiry*, 56:304-323.

Sutherland, E.H. 1940: 'The White Collar Criminal', *American Sociological Review*, 5:1-12.

Sutherland, E.H. 1949: *White Collar Crime*. New York: Dryden.

Sutherland, E.H. & Cressey, D. 1974: *Criminology*. Philadelphia: Lippincot.

Sykes, G. and Matza, D. 1957: 'Techniques of Neutralization', *American Sociological Review*, 22:664-670.

Tannenbaum, F. 1938: *Crime and the Community*. New York: Ginn.

Taylor, I., Walton, P. and Young, J. 1973: *The New Criminology: For a Social Theory of Deviance*. London: Routledge and Kegan Paul.

Wilkins, L.T. 1964: *Social Deviance: Social Policy, Action, and Research*. London: Tavistock Publications Ltd.

Wilson, J.Q. and Kelling, G. 1982: 'Broken Windows', *Atlantic Monthly*, March: 29-38.

Young, J. 1971: 'The Role of the Police as Amplifiers of Deviancy, Negotiators of Reality and Translators of Fantasy: Some Consequences of Our Present System of Drug Control as seen in Notting Hill.' In Cohen, S. (ed): *Images of Deviance*. Harmondsworth: Penguin Books, Ltd.

Young, J. 1987: 'The Tasks Facing a Realist Criminology', *Contemporary Crises*, 11(4):337-356.

Young, J. 1994: 'Incessant Chatter: Recent Paradigms in Criminology.' In Maguire, M. et. al. (eds) *The Oxford Handbook of Criminology*. Oxford: Clarendon Press.

Young, J. and Matthews R. (eds) 1992: *Rethinking Criminology: The Realist Debate*. London: Sage Publications.

Zehr, H. 1996: 'Justice Alternatives: A Restorative Perspective', *Imbizo*, Supplement:2-4.

Glossary

Abolitionism an approach to crime control which aims to diminish the role of the state by decriminalising certain offences

Altruistic suicide from Durkheim, suicide which results from a very high level of integration

Anomic suicide from Durkheim, suicide which results from a lack of regulation

Anomie a social condition in which norms are uncertain or lacking

Capital punishment the legal use of a sentence of death upon a convicted offender. Another term for the death penalty

Conflict theory broad term for theories (Marxism among them) which deny the prominence of value consensus in society and emphasise conflict between various groups

Conformism from Merton, the act of someone who accepts society's goals and the means to achieve them

Conservatism against liberalism, an ideology which emphasises the importance of traditional moral values and institutions such as the family, church and community for social order

Corporate crime a violation of a criminal law either by a company or by its executives, employees, or agents acting on behalf of and for the benefit of the corporation

Crime an act that breaks or violates a law

Criminal justice system the various agencies of 'justice', especially police, courts and prisons, whose goal it is to apprehend, convict, punish and rehabilitate law violators

Cultural deprivation the position of working-class children who are not socialised into middle-class standards by their families and find themselves at a disadvantage in schools

Deterrence an approach to crime control where the punishment is severe enough to discourage both individuals and the general public from committing crime

Deviance behaviour which violates social norms

Differential association the theory that crime, like any other form of behaviour, is learned through a process of association with others who communicate criminal values

Drift the way in which adolescents shift their behaviour from subterranean to mainstream values as they get older

Egoistic suicide from Durkheim, suicide which results from a lack of integration

Fatalistic suicide from Durkheim, suicide which results from an excess of regulation

Innovation from Merton, the way in which some individuals find new (sometimes illegal) ways to achieve the socially valued goals of society

Integration from Durkheim, the degree to which individuals form part of the community

Just deserts a policy for controlling crime which emphasises that punishment should be in proportion to the offence

Labelling an interactionist perspective which sees continued crime as a result of negative responses to those defined as criminal

Liberalism an ideology that views individuals as essentially the same and inherently good, with the same dignity, capable of restructuring society by means of their rational capacities

Master status an attribute which overshadows the other attributes of an individual and concentrates on the deviant (stigmatised) status

Neo-liberalism an economic policy which strongly emphasises the value of the free market

Primary deviance initial deviance often undertaken to deal with problems in day-to-day life

Rape sex through the use of force or the threat of force

Rate of crime the number of crimes committed during a year per 100 000 people

Rebellion from Merton, the act of someone who rejects society's goals and the means to achieve, and sets new goals and means

Regulation from Durkheim, the control which society exercises over an individual's actions

Rehabilitation the policy of reforming criminals through treatment and re-education

Restorative justice an approach to crime control where the aim is to restore community relationships through negotiation between the victim, the offender, members of the community and state officials

Retreatism from Merton, the act of someone who rejects both society's goals and the means to achieve them

Ritualism from Merton, the act of someone who ignores society's goals but focuses on the means instead

Secondary deviance deviant behaviour that results from official labelling and from association with others who have been labelled

Self-fulfilling prophecy where the expectation that something will happen makes it happen

Situational crime prevention a policy for controlling crime which emphasises the prevention of crime by limiting the opportunities for crime

Social policies government initiatives, programmes, and plans intended to address problems in society

Socialism an ideology which is critical of capitalism and hence favours egalitarianism, cooperation and rationalism in society

Status frustration a situation in which particularly working-class males find that their goal to achieve status in conventional society is blocked

Statutory rape rape without the use of force, often of under-age victims

Strain from Merton, the tension which arises when someone accepts society's goals but lacks the means to achieve them

Subculture the values and norms of a group of people which conflict with the mainstream values and norms in a society

Subterranean values values like aggression, adventure, thrill-seeking, in conflict with, and usually suppressed by, mainstream values but appearing at selected times and places

Suicide the killing of oneself

Target hardening the reduction in criminal opportunity, generally through the use of physical barriers, architectural design and enhanced security measures, of a particular location

Techniques of neutralisation ways in which individuals deny responsibility for their actions or deny that what they did was wrong

Underclass the lower end of the lower class

White-collar crime breaking the law by a person of respectability and high social status in the course of his or her work

Zero tolerance a policy to control crime which refers variously to getting tough on crime, clamping down on minor public order offences or curbing so-called incivilities

Index